Enjoy Your Life

Pursuing My Grandmother's Three Word Legacy

—— BY KIM SMITH ——

An Unbelievable Freedom® Book

This book is lovingly dedicated to my grandmother,
Lorraine Beatham

Gram, when you died, I imagined engraving your name on a bronze plaque. I wanted to mount it on a church pew or a park bench to symbolize that your legacy would live forever. Instead, I wrote books and I dedicated them to you. More than that, my life is dedicated to your memory. Your spirit is inscribed on the work I do in the world. I am your legacy.

Now the Lord is the Spirit, and where the Spirit of the Lord is, there is freedom.

2 CORINTHIANS 3:17

You see what's hidden under the surface
You see the beauty under the tarnish

You will find in fire what You call gold
You will find in fire what You can mold

Find me here in Your presence
I'm not leaving the same
Let Your refining fire
Purify me again
Let the weight of Your glory
Bring me back to my knees
O God come with revival
You can start it in me

From *Gold*, Jesus Culture featuring
Bryan and Katie Torwalt

Table of Contents

Preface

You're holding a book that was born when my grandmother died.

For nearly eight years, I've been starting and stopping, working and writing, hoping and healing. This book in your hands was a dream in my heart, now made real. This book is an answered prayer, but even more so, my life is an answered prayer. I am an answered prayer.

This preface makes promises to you, my readers, about why I wrote it and what I hope it will accomplish. When I hear the word "Promises", it calls up an image of the promises God has made to his children, as in, "God's promises are true" and "Believers can stand on His promises."

Central to these sacred promises is the idea that we can never and will never be separated from God's love. One thing I learned along my life's journey changed everything: I now understand how to receive God's love. Knowing I'll never be separated from God, believing it deeply into my cells, has created the expansive sense of freedom from which I live. God's love is the fuel that energizes my flow through the world.

This book makes one central pledge. I promise to explain how my grandmother taught me to receive God's love. With just 3 words and her example, she gave me everything I needed to experience and believe in Unbelievable Freedom.

I typed these pages over the late winter 2020 and early spring 2021. I love to think of someone reading this book in the future, needing to be reminded that this was months into the global Covid-19 pandemic that changed the world. This book was created in the context of life after strict lockdown, but in a world still limited by many restrictions. Like people around the world, the pandemic brought me into a deeper sense of spiritual surrender. My central image from lockdown is sitting cross-legged in a sunbeam, streaming the debut of Kari Jobe's "The Blessing" in my ears, feeling suffused with peace as joy replaced fear of death.

Practically speaking, change is in the air, too. We just moved to a new city, leaving a medium-sized house and yard with a copious burden of upkeep to occupy a small apartment with a river view - my personal "upper room." Since the move, I've spent more time praying and praising God than ever. My youngest is about to graduate from college and start her career in a big city south of here. A few weeks ago, I became a grandmother for the first time as my oldest and his wife welcomed their son. My fledgling grandmother-hood is another important piece of the puzzle.

A few months ago, eager to move "Gram's book" forward, I enrolled in a course on formal nonfiction book proposals. It taught how to create the document used by literary agents to approach publishers and sell book rights. I was so excited to get started. It was finally time to make this book real! The course was transparent about the fact that the publishing industry is a money-making business, and as such, there's motivation to secure only books that are "commercially compelling."

This brought the topic of marketability into sharp focus. Of course, I was aware of this reality; after all, I began my brief writing career in self-publishing precisely so I could bypass the need to follow the script. When we penned Unbelievable Freedom, I escaped the need to do anything except show up honestly and tell my story. It's one thing I can't get wrong, and I'm a big fan of failure-proof.

In buying book rights, publishers want to know, who are you and what's your platform look like? What's the size of your audience? In essence, tell us what you're famous for. While I'm far from famous, the answers about my platform had to do with weight loss success, built on a powerful story and some pretty unbelievable before-and-after photographs. Though I spent a few years promoting that transformation and encouraging others in developing similar habits, I began to feel called somewhere very different.

The further I ventured into the traditional publishing process, the more concerned I felt about going off course. The need to be marketable began to feel like a trap, one that would distort my dream book. I turned back to my first love, self publishing, to launch this book, the one I keep calling my first real book. Because of its connections to my grandmother, how it turns out is of sacred importance to me. This book can be real without an old-school publisher. If you're holding and reading it, it already is.

Knowing I've packaged and published a number of creative projects, those with sincere interest ask, what kind of book are you writing this time? This "book blob" I'm shaping right now- is it destined to become a memoir? Is it an instructive self-help book? Is it a spiritual book? I didn't know the precise response, and as my fingers strike the keys to form these words, I still don't.

This is a book that's about my grandmother, but not about my grandmother. It's a book that's about me, but also not about me. It is a book about God and what He can do in the life of a girl who stops running, turns to face Him, and surrenders to the joy and freedom she was made to experience.

Note: I refer to myself frequently as a girl in these pages, even though I'm a fully grown, proudly self-respecting woman. I claimed "Poster Girl for Contentment" as a moniker through a phase of my journey and I still identify with it, though layers of complexity have emerged in sustaining that status. I feel like more of a poster girl for God's grace. I acknowledge that self referencing as a girl isn't a choice all women make, but it's one that feels comfortable and aligned for me.

I now see that I couldn't write this book until I was ready to fully give God the glory for all that's happened since 2013 (well, since 1973, but we'll be focusing on the most recent eight years).

I spent a period casually referring to God in my public writing, speaking of my prayers here and there, but I did not want God in the spotlight. That has changed, and with it has come freedom to create a book exactly as He wants it to look, feel, and be. Each day that I write, I submit the process and the product to the Holy Spirit, and the words come.

My grandmother's role in my story comes via the way she showed up and stood in for God at so many critical junctures. At times I could not let myself believe God was for me, I believed she was for me. Her place comes in the way she loved me and how her light guided me through trials. It's in the words she spoke, Enjoy Your Life, words that reverberate in each of my days. My pursuit of what she meant by Enjoy Your Life brought me to a freedom I believe in.

My grandmother lived to be 95 years old, the final 25 of those as a widow dwelling solo in her cozy home (but because of her faith, never for a single moment alone!). Ultimately, she spent 66 continuous years in the same place, a house that loomed large in my development and still appears frequently in my dreams. I'll tell you more about this special place in the chapters that follow. It is a part of me forever.

As for Gram's life, it's a really simple straightforward story, typical for women of her time and place. She never drove a car. She only worked outside the home for roles in her church. She took good care of her family. She was beloved by her neighbors and her community. And at the end of her life, when she was unable to do more than be a loving presence on my sidelines, she planted seeds with her words, words that blossomed into the expansive sense of freedom that I can't stop praising.

Her seeds will bloom again when I publish this book. Retracing my own steps to create this road map, I will outline life enjoyment through Permission, Possibility, Participation and Praise. I'll share supporting material about Pruning, Perseverance, Pitfalls, and Pandiculation. Recognizing the dynamics in my life right now, I question whether it's too soon to publish yet, but it feels right. Realizing how much we're invited to stand in for God in the lives of others has transformed how I live in the world, especially as a new grandmother myself. It's allowed me to step into who I really am, the greatest feeling of freedom there is.

I've told pieces of my story in previous books, mostly notably the mini memoir I wrote with my husband Ryan, the original *Unbelievable Freedom*. That one focused on food, weight, and physical transformation, and putting it out there played a big role in my overall faith journey. It taught crucial lessons in terms of how to step forward, trust, and take bold action. I'm still proud of that book, and love hearing from those it impacted, but it left out what felt like my central truth, then and now.

The truth is this: I turned to God, after years of wandering and hiding and being afraid to invite Him in. When I stopped running, He picked up all my broken pieces and put me back together, in a better-than-ever way that still amazes me. Now, I live in a continuous, harmonious relationship with Him through the Holy Spirit. He healed my wounds, alleviated my fears, and gave me peace and joy beyond anything I thought was possible. I've dreamed about creating a book where I say just those words, those sentences you just read.

While all of that is true, it's worth telling the story of just how far I strayed in my teens, 20s and 30s, and how my grandmother was able, with three words, to lead me back to the place from which I was designed to live. I can honestly say that I feel like a restoration, just like projects where they bring old historic buildings back to life and people can see them as they were intended to be. When I look in the mirror, I see someone new yet familiar, as though I'm now the person I was always meant to be. Being my real self feels like freedom, and it allows me to overflow with joy in my family and in my work.

It's important to share that at the heart of my story is my decision to accept Jesus as savior. I have chosen to build my identity in Him and follow Him for the rest of my days. I shrug off the idea of being religious and in the same way, I hesitate to call this a Christian book because that brings up preconceived ideas. I have worked to get free of traps and boxes; I didn't do all that just to get tangled up by religiosity. Many people have been harmed and moved away from God due to the actions of so-called Christians. Religion isn't a meaningful word in my life, but freedom is.

This story has Jesus at its center, and I hope you're open to hearing what I have to say about His transformative work in me and in my life. I talk about it a lot. On a day-to-day basis, I'm navigating how to be in actual relationships with people disinterested in what Jesus has done for me. It's an unbelievable story and it tends to burst through everywhere. I'm in a how-can-I-be-silent phase of sharing my testimony.

There won't be much Scripture in the book but there will be snippets of praise song lyrics, all with a message like this: "He pulled me out of the pit. He put a song on my lips. He set my feet on the rock. He spoke a word to my heart" ("Be Strong", Jon Egan.) I'll share why these lyrics have been meaningful in my journey. There will be many mentions of God and Jesus, all of them exaltations. This is no different than the way I'd talk if we were meeting or having a conversation in person.

This book is for you if you're a new follower of Jesus or curious about how that journey may look and feel. It may inspire you if you've been in a lifelong battle with struggle and want to hear how a fellow struggler surrendered hers. Perhaps you had a special grandmother (or other significant person) who has passed on, and you enjoy stories that revere beloved figures. Maybe you just appreciate a good old-fashioned tale of transformation.

To you, the reader, here is my short list of additional promises about this book in your hands:

1. I promise to recount the details of my personal Enjoy-Your-Life Pursuit as I can recall them. I will tell the truth as I understand it, as clearly as I can express it. I have nothing to hide and if I did, I wouldn't be writing a book. I want to speak freely and it's why I chose to self-publish again.

2. I promise to be honest about what I don't know, which is quite a lot, especially about the Bible. This book contains a lot of "wow" over "how", which isn't everyone's cup of tea. I'm not a theologian nor am I a Biblical scholar. Neither fact has kept me from experiencing an intimate, ecstatic spiritual conversion. If I can enchant you with the "wow" of my story, that's a great place for God to show up and take over.

3. I promise to do my best to make this a book that sparks a shift. I intend for it to inspire change in your life, while acknowledging that my transformation occurred at the intersection of discipline and surrender. I call that intersection flow. Freedom and flow are fairly synonymous for me. I can share the discipline of what I do, but the surrender part is more mysterious. It's less easily explainable but equally real.

God called me to write a book that passes to others what He gave me through my grandmother. He crafted an ideal context in which I could do just that, and this is the result.

Enjoy the book! Enjoy Your Life!

CHAPTER 1

Pursuit

The House That Built Me

Picture this: A quiet street in Brewer, Maine, formerly a dirt road nestled amongst cow pastures but now smoothly paved. A white wood-frame cape-style house like thousands of others around New England. Inside the house, a little girl of about 5 stands at the edge of the living room on a hot-air register, its heated blast causing her blonde hair and her nightgown to billow simultaneously. Her eyes are closed; her face is peaceful with just a hint of a smile. The harmonious hum of her grandparents working together emanates from the kitchen nearby. She feels enveloped in warmth, in safety, in love. It feels like freedom.

The little girl is me, and that feeling of freedom will be relatively hard to find over the 35 years that come after this scene. My story begins inside the walls of my grandparents' house, a safe haven that would remain virtually unchanged over dozens of visits in my first 40 years of life.

My grandparents built the place right after World War II and moved in with their two small children, the younger my father. My grandmother proceeded to live her life from its rooms until her death in 2013. My earliest memories took place there. The times I felt most safe, most secure, most happy occurred inside its walls. I can't talk about who I am without thinking of it. "The House That Built Me" is a country song by Miranda Lambert that resonated when it was a current hit and it still does. If my grandmother was a stand-in for God, her home was a stand-in for Heaven.

I'm writing this book at the age of 47. Born in 1973, I grew up with a younger brother and sister. Both sets of our grandparents lived nearby. I was educated in public schools, exposed to Catholic mass and CCD on Sundays. My parents divorced when I was in my early teens and both quickly remarried. On that note, I've also been married twice. During my first marriage in my early 20s, I gave birth to two babies, one boy and one girl, now young adults. My son just started a family of his own and my daughter is graduating from college.

I've always understood that motherhood is a divine calling. I accept that every good and perfect gift is from above. Unfortunately, instead of wearing that truth like a crown, I half-turned away from it, forsaking joy in favor of frustration. I felt cheated by my perceived failure to meet the world's definition of success in other areas of life.

Though it's tough to admit, I didn't feel deserving of such beautiful children, questioning whether God knew what He was doing in giving them to me. I choose not to regret anything but easily envision how motherhood would have been different if I'd reveled in my blessing instead of resenting what I hadn't been given.

My current marriage, now in its 18th year, is the most challenging and deeply satisfying relationship of my life. I believe marriage should be both, though I prefer the easy parts to the tough ones. My husband Ryan is a wonderful man, one who works hard and keeps his word. He helped me put our first book into the world and has consistently supported me during the trials detailed in these pages. I'll leave it to him whether he ever wants to share his faith journey or the ways mine has impacted him. They say 'have a marriage that feels like the safest place on Earth.' I do. While this book isn't about Ryan, he is a hero in my story.

You could say I'm a smart cookie. I've been accused of being bright all my life, and I acknowledge my intellectual abilities, but I've wondered what it means. It has felt at times like a set up, blessed with potential so easily squandered. Over a span of 16 years, I earned three college degrees, a Bachelors and two Masters, and I carry the debt that accompanies so much higher education. I've worked a number of part-time and full-time jobs. I dreamed (or maybe just fantasized?) about being a teacher, a school guidance counselor, a medical social worker, a child-birth coach, a sign language interpreter, and more.

What do all those positions have in common? They're all places where I believed I could make myself of unique and special use. I've struggled with career direction, with indecision and neurosis, with a near-obsession with needing to be beneficial in this world. I've struggled to form lasting friendships, especially as an adult. I've struggled with food and I've struggled with my weight. I've struggled in general.

As a child who performed well in school, I developed an early identification with my intellect, maybe even an over-identification with it. I wanted to analyze things and figure them out, force them to make sense in my brain. I've learned that with faith, a pure heart is more important than a keen intellect. This is why the Bible talks about embracing childlike wonder - there is freedom in the trusting of continual uncertainty. For most of my life, I lived with so much fear that I clung to illusions of certainty and control. Surrendering these illusions is my continual pursuit.

At the same time that I was over-identifying with my intellect, I was under-identifying with my emotions. I possess many traits of the so-called Highly Sensitive Person; I recognize these in my memories of childhood and they're still with me as an adult. Experiencing emotions in a deep way is a part of my design, but early on, I learned to repress rather than express. Now, I embrace my keen ability to express myself, and I readily reveal my thoughts and feelings. I even write books about them. I see how suppressing my emotions made it difficult for others to support me, fueling a cycle of feeling frustrated, fearful, dissatisfied, and distrusting.

This litany of my life's events may seem a bit gloomy, but it's shared to illustrate that there's nothing noteworthy about me. I've had my highs and my lows, and I know I'm not unique or alone in my struggles. Unless we've lived inside a bubble, each one of us has experienced heartache and disappointment. Actually, living inside a bubble would be its own trial, and I'll say more about that later.

I could write a whole book about my struggles, but I don't want to do that. I could tell you more about childhood anxiety, about believing that my special needs were a burden to my parents. They had a troubled marriage and seemed dissatisfied with their lives; like so many children, the belief that I was at fault created a slow-healing wound.

I could write about the heartbreak of my young divorce. I could tell you about the disappointment that grew into a smothering sense of failure as a number of career paths didn't work out. I could share my struggles with focus that created struggles with time management and self care. I could write (actually, I've already written a lot) about a compulsion for junk food and the weight gain that brought me into the category of morbid obesity.

The most important thing to know is that all of the above combined like the ingredients in a recipe, the full formula for building a personal mire of misery.

The Mire That I Built

The foundation of the Mire that later contained me was constructed in my childhood. For reasons He knows best, God designed me with a deep observational nature that meant I seemed unnaturally serious to those around me. I grew up feeling and thinking deeply, and it showed.

I remember feeling sour, then being chided for acting it. I detested being called a sourpuss. In childhood photos, I'm seen frowning, scowling, or hunching away from someone's hug. I recall my father calling me "Crumbly" a funny twist on Kimberly, as though I was a broken thing falling apart. With full recognition that adults don't set out to create false narratives in impressionable young minds, from early memory, that is what was happening. I was soaking up a story about my sourness.

I remember overhearing talk about how different I was from my younger brother, how sweet-natured and jolly he was. Whatever alchemy occurred between my natural temperament and the power of the narrative, I can admit I was sour. I remember disliking going to the ocean, slimy seaweed everywhere, the strong scent of the beach at low tide. What does one do with a child who is unhappy at the beach?

I remember sulking and pouting, sometimes bitterly complaining. I remember disliking gifts that were given to me as a child, and it's likely I didn't do a good job concealing it. I remember feeling very misunderstood by the world and the people around me. I struggled to receive attention or affection from others.

I can acknowledge how easily adults plant these seeds because as I look back, it's likely that I made similar remarks comparing my son to my daughter. My daughter is my grandmother's namesake and I desperately wanted to claim for her my Gram's sunshiny disposition. I spoke it out over her life boldly, but for all the love and concern I poured into my son, I didn't give much thought to how my description of his sister impacted him. He's doing great in his young adulthood, and I hope he'll reject any sense of lacking because he is different from his sister. His sensitive and reactive temperament is more like mine, and that caused me to worry much more about him as he grew.

As I moved through my school years, I learned to force a smile and hide from the world how sour I felt. The sense in my mind was that if you wanted acceptance from others, you should not seem unhappy. I got better at pretending. You should try to be whatever they seem to want or expect. I did my best. We all do.

For the sake of chronology, let's use this as the landmark: 40. By the eve of my 40th birthday, I was deeply embedded in what I call The Mire.

I first described this mythical place in my second book *Unmired*. In the opening of that book, I painted a visual using my best Maine Girl imagery. Spring is mud season in Maine so I used its fresh, wet, clay-like texture to illustrate what it was like to be stuck there. In truth, the Mire was also dry and barren like a desert. I have to be grateful for that, because my thirst for God blossomed out of that dusty ground.

When I speak about being in the Mire, it coincides with the part of my life that I spent in unbelief, when I believed God was FOR REAL but God was not FOR ME. All time spent believing that I was separated from God was mired time. The most pervasive aspect of the Mire was the hum of discontented frustration. I wanted out but had no idea which way to go. Struggle was the air I breathed, yet I railed against it, knowing everything should be flowing more easily, that I wasn't made to struggle so hard.

Woven into this Mire were layers of resentment. Resentment became the foundation of and the fuel for the Mire. Resentment was the obstacle between me and God. Resentment was both the cause and effect of the Mire. Confused yet?

From the time I was a kid, I watched other people closely, convinced they'd been given gifts or marked for joy that I'd been denied. I tried way too hard to be happy; the effort became its own trap. Ever had a dream where you run but make no progress at all? My frustration felt like that. Eventually, for the survival of my psyche, I stopped my thrashing and moved into quiet despair.

From deep inside the Mire, I watched the world around me sparkle, moving at a brilliant and beautiful pace while I felt destined to slog through invisible wet cement. Things that came easily to others didn't flow to me and I could not figure out why. Was it self sabotage? Was it a curse? Was it my fault or was it someone else's? It was impossible to discern from inside the Mire. It is a fundamentally foggy place where nothing makes sense. There isn't much light so there's no clarity.

In many ways, the first 40 years of my life were about slowly, systematically creating and maintaining my Mire, though I was scarcely aware of any personal agency. Life felt like it was happening to me. The harder I tried to be successful and happy, the more elusive it became, until it seemed certain that I was doomed.

Becoming Unmired

Fortunately, if the Mire was a curse, it was one meant to be broken.

As my 20s and 30s unfolded, the pattern of frustration and disappointment continued. I pitied myself, then scolded myself for the pity, ashamed of the pathetic nature of this loop. I felt alone, devoid of help and support, yet I behaved in ways that alienated others, kept them at bay, and made certain they couldn't see or understand my struggle. I ached for connection and my desperation repelled the things that would invite its satisfactions into my day-to-day life. I was ambivalence personified.

I dealt with life in my Mire through in the most dysfunctional ways - I viewed others (and myself) with harsh judgment, I complained and ruminated, I agonized and overthought, I avoided taking action at all costs.

A key theme in the years where I struggled, spun my wheels, and dug deeper into my personal Mire: a scarcity of solid coping skills. I held my Mire together with my bad habits. I didn't really want to develop coping skills because then I'd be accountable to use them and to move forward, out of the Mire and into the world. I was scared, and I suppose I just wasn't ready.

From where I am now, I know that coping skills come in two categories: worldly and spiritual. The worldly ones can be healthy, supportive and self-serving (exercise, nourishing food, deep breathing, journaling, creative hobbies) or unhealthy and self-defeating (overeating, drinking too much alcohol, using drugs, numbing/distracting with technology).

I used to lack all coping skills, but now, I have a collection of useful ones in both camps. I've made great progress by increasing the quality and decreasing the quantity of the food I eat. I walk several miles most days, I get great sleep, and I've switched to natural alternatives for most products I use on my body and in my home.

However, spiritual coping skills are in a class of their own, and I turn to them the most. These are praying, worship and praise, singing, reading the Bible, acts of service dedicated to God, etc. The most important spiritual coping skill is active belief. We must believe that God is with us, He is for us, He will never abandon us, His promises are true. As I continually surrender my unbelief, my ability to cope with all of life's stressors improves. My faith reminds me of my lack of control, and as it does, I feel deeper freedom. Everything streamlines. Everything flows. Lord, less of me, more of You.

I decided not to write a traditional memoir because my actual story didn't seem that interesting to me. I want to be clear, though, that it isn't because I believe the circumstances are unimportant. They are critical to my life. They broke me and made me again. God was using every single bit of it, every step of the way. I honor each piece of my life's journey that brought me to this point.

I acknowledge the same about your heartache and striving, past and present. If you're reading this as a struggler, know that your struggle can be redeemed. All of the stumbles, struggles, shames, mistakes, every shred and crumb can be used by

God. You can surrender it all to Him and ask Him to make it a part of your redemption story. He will.

When I look at the bundle of circumstances that comprised my Mire, I believe some parts were anointed, designated by God as part of His plan for my life, and others were redeemed by Him after I went way (way, way, way) astray and needed rescuing. Writing from my current vantage point, I can see that in each and every season, God was using other people to stand in. He used my grandmother as well as many others. He was drawing me to Him. As they say, His fingerprints are all over it.

Had I not been in a Mire, I could not have become Unmired. If I had not become Unmired, I would not be standing on this particular rooftop shouting this unique testimony. And because of what He has spoken to my heart, I'm confident God will use this testimony to change someone's life...maybe yours.

In each of the sub-threads of my life is a through-line: sour resentment and self-pity that led me away from the truth of who God is and who God created me to be. Resentment became my maladaptive, self-destructive default. Resentment was a way of hiding, a way of blaming, a twisted way of protecting myself. When resentment is my lens, I have the strangely soothing "success" of continually finding evidence for more. I find evidence of how hard things are, how unfair life is, how disappointing other people are. It steals my joy and it becomes a massive obstacle to my freedom.

At this point, my goal for the rest of my time on Earth is never to stray far enough from God to become mired all over again. I intend to access the Holy Spirit actively so that I flow Unmired through all that is to come. So far, it is proving to be an excellent strategy. Access to God through the Holy Spirit is immediate and the resources He gives are abundant. Everything may not be perfect, but I am free.

This book is all about how I learned to do this, and I hope to share it in a way that inspires you to Enjoy Your Life by staying Unmired, too.

CHAPTER 2

Petition

Oasis of Tranquility

I've always described my grandmother's home as an oasis of tranquility. That is simply the best way to describe what it represented for me. While we will never see or understand Heaven on this side of it, Gram's home was pretty close, free from stress and strain, full of warmth and generosity.

Though I loved my grandfather dearly, my grandmother was the reason for this generous description. She was the source of the tranquility. A seemingly endless peace radiated from her. On the movie screen in my mind, from my earliest memory, she is softly luminous. In reality, I know this illumination was invisible to the eye, but I could feel it as much as I felt the warmth of the sun. Her glow was felt by others, too. People were drawn to the soft light of her loving attention. Over and over, people who knew my grandmother have told me, "There was just something about her!" Indeed there was. We knew her by her love and her light.

She was always humming or singing, that image of the person with such deep contentment that it leaks or spills out as music. Old hymns, little ditties like "I Love You, a Bushel and a Peck" or "Pease Porridge Hot", some song about a Jack o'lantern that springs back into my mind when someone claims there are no Halloween songs.

When I slept over at my grandparents' house, I'd stand on that hot air register in the morning, my flannel nightie billowing around my legs. Too young to understand the mechanics of a forced hot-air furnace, it seemed this heat emanated from a magical place, its ticklish pleasure never to end. It brought a sense of deep contentment that I can still feel if I close my eyes.

With those same closed eyes, I can see Gram now, puttering, softly humming as she moves through the rooms of her cozy house. When I was in her presence, I felt secure, whether I was standing on a blasting hot air register or not. When she was nearby, all was well. In this way, during my childhood and most of my adulthood, she stood in for God. Her approving, loving energy flowed lavishly like God's, a well that could not and would not run dry.

My relationship with my grandmother was my stable constant. She was always there, turning and wiping her hands on her apron as I stepped up into her kitchen. Knowing she was in her home, accessible if I needed her, grounded me during years of tumultuous change. She wasn't my confidante or someone to whom I told secrets. I didn't come to her to unload the details of my jobs imploding or my first marriage falling apart. Maybe some relate to their grandmothers that way but not me.

I didn't come to her for advice; I came to her for acceptance. She was not an advice giver, anyway; she was never once a "finger wagger." I can't even call her a role model in the sense of striving to shape my own life based on hers, at least back then. I can guess how she felt about my life choices but I can't confirm any of it based on what she said or did. She never judged me. She simply loved me.

More than that, she delighted in me. I remember hearing that every child should have someone whose face lights up when they walk into the room. For me, that person was my grandmother. It was true when I was 7 and just as apparent when I was 37. My children were the blessed recipients of the same loving delight. "Delighting" was central to her job description as a grandmother, brightening when she saw us, clutching her hands together in pleasure. She made me feel like the shining star of the show, and that's something I desperately needed. At 7 and at 37.

Sometimes I talk about my grandmother's importance in my life and I'm asked questions about her that I can't answer. While I rue the fact that I didn't learn more about her, gather up more of her stories and anecdotes and ideas, I know why I didn't. It's because every time I was with her, she was focused on me, asking about me, my interests, my friends. She listened with rapt attention, hanging on my words. They say, make everybody feel like a somebody. She made me feel like more than a somebody. She made me feel fascinating.

In the last few years of my grandmother's life, as she moved from her late 80s into her 90s, I know she saw my struggle. The obvious physical aspect makes it undeniable - who has a granddaughter who gains nearly 100 pounds without them noticing? From her vantage point, with a lifetime of wisdom under her belt, she got it...life wasn't working out the way I'd hoped. She may not have been worldly but she was wise. She understood much of my struggle was a waste of energy, yet she gave me grace.

My Gram understood the importance of preserving people's dignity. She always focused on the positive in every interaction. She knew that I needed to give my struggle to God, but that was never preached. Any conversation about my life was touched by her encouragement and gentle grace. Like her house, it made me feel safe to be under her loving, accepting gaze.

A Humble and Holy Petition

In those final years, I'd see Gram on the major holidays and a handful of summer occasions, when we'd gather in her backyard or another outdoor spot for a picnic. Never enough, and just like the cliches insist, I wish that we'd gotten together far more often. Until Heaven, I will have to see her in my dreams.

Always petite, Gram became even tinier as she moved into her 90s. Right until the end, she stayed vibrant and engaged. Her mind was sharp. Her body shrank and her spirit expanded, her loving energy growing larger and larger.

When it was time to part ways at the close of our visits, whether it was at her door as I headed to my car, or because my father was (rather impatiently) waiting to escort her to his, she would lean toward me, eyes twinkling. I'd bend slightly to hear what she was going to say. Sometimes she'd reach out and gently squeeze my arm just above the elbow as she said:

"Enjoy your life!"

These three words became her standard way of closing the visit, simple and unpretentious, like "Have a nice day!" But the first few times, the words landed on my spirit with a thud, triggering a warm flush of shame. I can admit it now. I was embarrassed that my grandmother could see my Mire despite my effort to hide. Looking back, I understand how clearly she must have seen me, how my forced smile failed to fool her.

She knew yet she never seemed worried. Why hadn't she fretted? Why hadn't she tried to fix it? She truly believed, and knew worry is a symptom of unbelief. She trusted that God had me, and she was right.

Enjoy Your Life. Enjoy Your Life. Enjoy Your Life.

I loved her for saying those words but I didn't know how to receive them. I knew they were meant with warmth and kindness, but they were mystifying. Enjoy life? Mine? Maybe she didn't realize just what a mess it was, what a mess I was. Maybe if she saw the full, real deal of my life, she wouldn't have bothered to utter them. That's what I thought back then.

Three small words as humble and unassuming as my grandmother herself. Short, sweet, and powerful, they were more than a wish.

I came to understand these words as a holy petition.

After Gram died, there were some blurry, hard-to-recall weeks. I remember that her funeral was simple and beautiful, her former choir-mates at the front of church singing "It Is Well" while I wept inconsolably. She was cremated and her remains placed in the plot where my grandfather had been buried 25 years earlier. I never thought to ask for any of the "cremains" to scatter or put inside a locket. I could scarcely catch my breath, let alone think ahead in that way.

As the shock of grief started to wear off, her words began to return to me. During the culling of six decades of detritus packed into her house's nooks and crannies, they echoed in my ears anew. Enjoy Your Life. What had she meant, really? What did she want me to know, to feel?

I came to see the Enjoy Your Life petition almost like a puzzle, one that made me curious for the first time in so long. Curiosity jarred me out of my lethargy. I was awake, and I had the first clue in a long-overdue treasure hunt. There was a clue but no map, certainly no secret decoder ring. I had to mine for gemstones if I wanted to interpret her message from beyond the grave.

So as the fog lifted, there she was. She was still with me, beckoning. With those words, she guided me onward as I stumbled into the reality of my life after her death. She was teaching me still, showing me just how much she'd been a stand-in for God Himself. There was hope in the idea that she would always be with me through her words. Within the most intense grief I'd ever experienced, there was growing comfort in the feeling I could do it - learn to enjoy my life - and I would do it FOR her.

She was not just petitioning me when she said Enjoy Your Life, though she'd spoken the words directly to my ear. She was petitioning all of Heaven itself. They were three small words out of the multitudes I believe she'd prayed for me, beginning before I came out of the womb and for the 40 years that followed. "Your grandmother's prayers are still protecting you" is a sentiment from a popular Internet meme, but I believe to my core that it's the truth of my life. My grandmother's prayers are still protecting me. My grandmother's prayers are still setting me free.

Because of what God has revealed to me about my grandmother and her faith, I believe she spoke bold prayers over my life from my earliest days, and that those prayers were indeed heard. They were made with a pure heart to a God who listens, meaning those prayers created intercession. Those prayers activated my spiritual DNA, showed me God's truth, and led me home to Him. Her words reverberate as I pray actively over my grandson's life now, reverberating echoes of grace. In my new grandmother-hood, I feel more aligned with her spirit than ever.

People who knew my grandmother longer than I confirm she's someone who didn't talk much about her faith, but rather, she lived her faith. She attended the same church from young childhood to her 90s. She sang hymns with her beloved choir and in her beloved kitchen. Her Bible was never far from her reach. Her deep belief guided her steps, including in her divine assignment as grandmother to a struggling young girl-turned-woman. I know it.

She lived her life with her eyes on Jesus, and that brought a deep contentment that drew others to her magnetically. When she entered the room, there was a shift in the spiritual atmosphere. I always knew in my heart that she was extra special, so being her granddaughter made me special. When she died, a panicky thought rose up: how can I be special now that she's gone?

Actually, I feel that her passing is what fully activated her spiritual legacy within me, causing me to finally lift my head, look squarely at who I was supposed to become. When I finally faced the fact that I had to carry on here without her, I knew it was time. I became consumed with finally being freed from the Mire.

Gone From My Sight

The moment when I accepted that she was truly gone happened a few days after her death. I stood in her living room, my back toward the front windows, looking at her old rocking chair standing motionless in a sunbeam. My beloved hot air register was a few feet away but silent, the day unseasonably warm for October, no need for the big furnace to be cranking.

Gram's Bible and a paperback novel sat on the side table next to her emery boards and a tube of hand cream. The room was a picture of stillness but for one exception: her wall clock. It ticked out loud, insistent clicks, each one widening the divide between the time we'd both been alive and now. I wanted the clicking to stop. I didn't want her to join the list of those loved ones who'd "died a long time ago", yet the clock was reminding me that span was getting bigger with every breath.

Gram had been in this room, in that chair, a handful of weeks earlier, humming and singing, handling those familiar items on the table. Now she was absent. She was completely gone from my sight. I couldn't even feel her presence. I couldn't feel much of anything. I felt numb. I felt utterly alone but within my despair was a cry for rescue. It began with faint, tiny prayers to believe I would see her again in Heaven.

Still, I have to ask why her death wrecked me like it did. I had been preparing for this moment for a long time. I was a grown woman whose grandmother had essentially died of old age, cognitive abilities intact. At her passing, she'd been deeply accepting that this was her time. She'd prayed not to require long term nursing care, and as she began to slip away, she was relieved that the prayer had been answered. From many viewpoints, her peaceful passing was a cause for rejoicing, or maybe it could have been if my faith had been solid. Instead, I was bereft.

My efforts to prepare myself to lose her had been diligent but feeble, and seemingly hadn't helped much at all. I'd been slowly saying goodbye to my grandmother for years. I had driven down the interstate listening to country music, crying about her inevitable death, while she was still alive and well. I'm no expert on how anticipatory grief functions but I know it didn't stop me from being knocked to the ground. The tidal wave of grief is what forced me to finally surrender. After years of quiet but swelling struggle, Gram's death brought me to my knees.

I regressed into a child-like irrationality, wanting to thrash and tantrum, angry that she had been taken away from me. I remember speaking on the phone to my father's cousin from out of state who called for an update. When I informed him that Gram had passed, he replied with a tone of celebration, "Praise the Lord! Aunt Lorraine has been promoted to the Glory!"

I wanted to be appropriate, so on the surface, I was polite to this sweet gentleman I barely know. On the inside, his gleeful words made me fume. How dare he act like this was a good thing! I didn't want my Gram to be elevated to the so-called Glory; I wanted her right here. I need her as a balm to soothe the difficult parts of my life.

Orphan is the term for someone whose parents have both died. There's no equivalent term for a person who lacks a living grandmother, but if there were, it would have been the identity I claimed following Gram's death. I threw myself into mourning as my focus. I talked about her to anyone who would listen. I played sad songs and made myself cry on purpose. I wept until my face was chapped.

Practically speaking, I had to figure out how to move through the world without her. I was an adult and I had responsibilities; I couldn't just crawl into a hole. Plus, I already felt I was in one. What I needed was to climb up and out, but due to everything that had gone wrong up to that point, I had no idea what to do next. I didn't trust myself. I didn't trust God. How could I redeem myself? How could I escape the Mire?

I was lost but finally, I was ready to seek in earnest. I took the first step, drawn to venture outdoors into the fresh air to explore. For the first time in many years, I took some genuinely deep breaths. I looked for signs of her in the birds, the butterflies, the wind on my face. I needed an indication she was still real...somewhere. Wow, it was beautiful out there in nature. Where had this been all those years? I felt like I was waking up from a coma, suddenly smack dab in the middle of that brilliant world I'd watched from inside the mire.

Let's review my life at that moment. I was sad and anxious most of the time, my physical health was deteriorating, my marriage was limping along, my heart-desired career was nonexistent. My children were doing well but nearly grown and about to leave me. That thought alone evoked panic. Like many mothers facing the empty nest, I believed they were the best part of my life and soon to be gone from it, leaving me with nothing.

I wished I could ask my grandmother where I should start. Which of these messes should I start to clean up first? Should I begin with what seemed most manageable, or was it better to tackle the scariest parts head on? I didn't even have a guess what Gram might advise. I did not know what she wanted me to do.

I only knew that she wanted me to enjoy my life, and that sparked what I now know was sacred curiosity. I had to figure out what that meant, how it looked, what to do. And honestly, that was the ideal place to start. It was the point from which to embark on the personal scavenger hunt I now refer to as my Enjoy-Your-Life Experiment.

CHAPTER 3

Permission

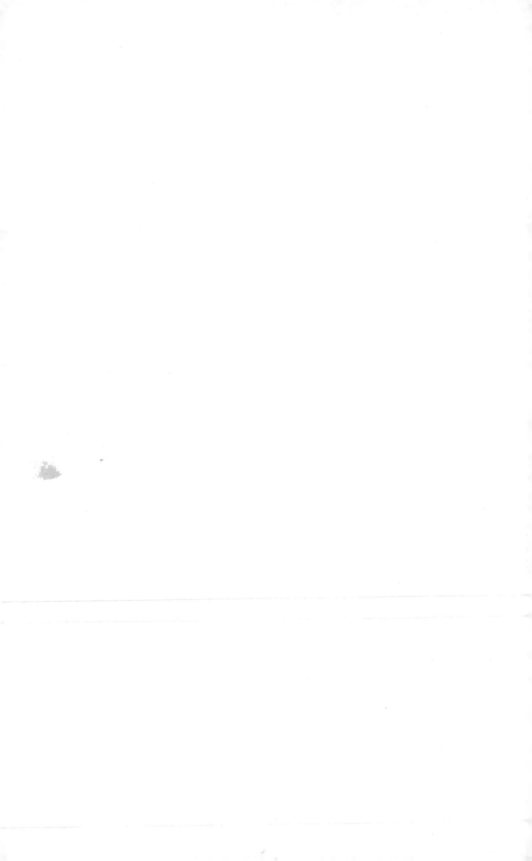

My Permission Slip

ENJOY YOUR LIFE created permission: permission to change, permission to grow, permission to admit my struggle, permission to approach God. It brought permission to turn to Him with my pain, with my questions, with my desire to believe in a new, deeper way.

Enjoy Your Life created permission to admit what I'd been pretending not to know: that I wasn't enjoying my life at all. I was empty without God, but I hadn't wanted anyone to know that. I felt bad that my kids didn't have a happy mom. I wanted so much to be happy for them, and felt guilty that I wasn't. It was a vicious cycle until Gram's words intervened.

In every section of this book, I'm going to be tempted to say: this part is really important. They all are. Each portion of the pursuit was important because it led to the next one, and they all fit together in a continuous flow.

Not exactly an instantaneous lightbulb going off, but the words started to illuminate, to slowly transform in their power. Yes, they were originally received with a bit of dread and a deep sigh of resignation, because I was interpreting them on my own. We never had a single conversation about why she was saying it. I am not sure what I'd have asked, had I been given a chance to do so.

Maybe it would have gone like this: Enjoy? MY life? Gram, have you seen it? I've messed up everything I've tried to do. Changed majors, spun my wheels, failed to get a job out of college. Married young with stubborn insistence that I knew what I was doing, blundered it so badly that I knew no way to go backward or forward, couldn't get out without imploding the entire thing. Second shot at marriage was met with many of the same struggles and inabilities to communicate.

Gram, in my 20s and 30s, I got more chances and blew those, too. You saw me stuffing down my feelings as I stuffed my face. You saw the pounds pile on. But all the while your eyes were twinkling, you were saying those 3 words firmly, as though you knew it was possible and that I was capable. As though you knew that I was completely deserving and trusted that I'd know it, too.

I guess that imagined conversation is all I really need to have. The words had a purpose and she handed them off for me to use. With her death, she'd left them behind like an inheritance.

She didn't leave them so I could just shrug them off. She gave them to me as a gift so I had to figure out what this life enjoyment thing might look like. I had to unravel it, spread it out on a table, examine it from every angle. At the outset of a scavenger hunt, you start with one clue and here was mine.

Even with a clue in hand, I was at a bit of a loss. What was I supposed to do now? What had she left me for instructions? As I've shared, she was not a now-you-listen-to-me type of finger wagging grandmother. She lived and loved and let God handle the rest. There was very little I could fall back on in terms of what she expected or what she'd told me I should do.

Lighthearted as those words sound, I knew this was serious business. My Gram was incapable of pretense and didn't play games with people. She was genuinely warm. She was as loving as anyone I'd been privileged to meet, and she is the one who said Enjoy Your Life to me. Directly. Repeatedly. For years. *It meant something.*

And there was another ugly layer to what I was pretending not to know: I wasn't enjoying my life because I wouldn't let myself. Because I was doing things every day that made me feel lousy, flat-out sabotaging myself. Because I was holding people at bay, stubbornly hiding, wrapped up in shame and fear like a security blanket.

It was like the years I spent raising my children, the best work I ever did. I refused to ask for or accept much help, and that made it so hard. It isn't that there was no happiness, but that I held myself back from experiencing the fullness of joy. I wanted it but I didn't know how or didn't dare. I took the weight of everything that went wrong squarely onto my own shoulders. I parented without God in my perception of the equation (He was there!) and this made it so much harder than it needed to be.

I didn't drink my first cup of coffee until I was 30, after both kids had reached school age. This means that I parented them through infancy and toddlerhood... uncaffeinated. As a grateful (and carefully intentional) user of caffeine now, I can attest that those years would have been easier caffeinated. The magical energizing effects of caffeine are for the body what the magical energizing effects of God are for the spirit. While I managed without, I believe parenting would have been easier and more joyful with reliance on God and submission to His will as a conscious process.

Even as I can acknowledge that I didn't pray enough, relinquish illusions of control enough, seek spiritual support enough, I knew on some level that being a Mom was an active co-creation with God. It was a first glimpse into what it feels like to really participate actively with Spirit. It's why I mourned the idea of it ending when the empty nest loomed, and how I'd eventually understand participation later on.

But permission had to come first, and Gram's Enjoy Your Life petition is what sparked the shift. Once I admitted I wasn't enjoying my life, things began to change. Everything in my story links back to this moment in time. We've all heard about the importance of getting out of our own way, that the only thing holding us back is ourselves. When I review my unfolding Enjoy-Your-Life Experiment, permission is THE entry point.

From inside the Mire, it took time to understand that Gram's passing had opened a window. Through that window, a fresh breeze began to flow. She had signed and delivered my permission slip.

God's Refrigerator

I sometimes call this, "the moment I realized I was on God's refrigerator." That language came later, spoken in the context of a business development course I was taking, quoted from the course leader's own rabbi. I don't know when or how the image came to him. But honestly, the impetus and origin of my Enjoy-Your-Life Pursuit was born of the realization that I am on God's refrigerator, figuratively.

I was literally on Gram's refrigerator - there were reminders and representations of me peppered all over her house, the spaces through which she moved every day.

Digging through the hoard that was my grandmother's accumulated possessions, the souvenirs, the stuff that had made its way into the house over 66 years of residence. In my mind, I picture it like time-lapse photography, the 1940s flowing into the 50s and 60s, her children growing up, then the 70s and 80s, the grandchildren began to fill the space, and finally the 90s through the time of her death in 2013. Things come in, purchased and gifted, tidbits of a life. They make their way in the door and up the stairs, onto shelves and into closets, never to move again.

And sprinkled amongst this stuff? Me. Photograph upon photograph. My childhood drawings and my report cards. A once purple mimeograph now faded to pale lavender, a newsletter from my days at The Hilltop School, a reference to "Kimberly" noted in a lower corner. Numerous honor roll listings clipped from the newspaper. How many times had she picked these things up? Why had she kept them for so long? By the time I found them during my grieving, I was heavy in body and spirit. As I wondered how to redeem my misspent life, they were a sure sign.

My grandmother saw me. She cherished me. She delighted in me. And it was the beginning of understanding that God has the same orientation. The same delight. The same radical love for me that would cause Him to fasten my image to the equivalent of a refrigerator, though I don't know that Heaven has appliances or electricity. It's a metaphor and it's a God thing, a love thing.

And so my pursuit of life enjoyment began with the knowledge that I truly was special, that I was already Divine, and I was deserving of enjoying it all. I was worthy. I had permission, even a petition, to enjoy my life.

I started this section with my big disclaimer about importance because NONE of the rest of my transformation could have happened without this shift in attitude, in identity, in belief.

Years of hearing Enjoy Your Life was an anointing of sorts, my grandmother pouring subtle energy onto me over and over, applying layers that built up until they woke me up. Once she was gone, I started to see what she'd been saying all along: I am worthy of enjoying life, and I am capable of it, so let's get to it.

While I could write several more pages about changing my lifestyle, eating less often, eating different kinds of foods, moving my body in new ways, that's not really the point. The point is that I embraced God and as I did, I had to embrace my body as a temple of His Holy Spirit. Freedom from struggles with food and weight emerged as I claimed the truth of who and what God created me to be. I know He didn't create me for struggle, and in that context, it was and is easier to take each day's choices as they come.

With gentleness toward self, struggle has no opposing force. I'm able to release the energy of struggle from decisions around self care and wellness. It doesn't mean I never get it wrong. I still have days where I end up with a stomach ache from indulging in too many scones, but when I do, it doesn't mire me.

The practice I now call digestive rest (previously referred to as 'intermittent fasting') has become a sacred daily ritual, my time to lean in and hear God's voice more clearly in the stillness of a calm and quieted digestive tract. When I'm fasting, I can be dependent on God for all my sustenance. I feel empty and clean on the inside, purified, and this is a foundation for my spiritual refinement.

This practice has also supported deep physical healing, without a doubt, and that is an important part of my story. It is a portion of my testimony. My weight loss and recovery from disease reinforces everything else that has shifted within me. Any downplaying of my weight loss story now is simply my attempt to give credit where it's due.

The fasting-focused aspects of my story exist in the original book called *Unbelievable Freedom*, and the naming of that book is a God thing, too. Even then, as I typed out the story of how I changed my attitude and identity with regard to food, what was in my heart was the power of what God was doing in me. It was surrendering my unbelief (or my wobbly, half-belief) in God that brought me unbelievable freedom, once I truly believed. I wanted the world to know it was all for God's glory but I wasn't ready to say it on those pages.

Now I've given myself permission to tell that part of the story, too.

Give yourself permission to Enjoy Your Life.

CHAPTER 4

Possibility

Believing in Life Enjoyment

ENJOY YOUR LIFE created an expansive sense of possibility in my life. I'd grown up feeling sour, like someone who didn't know how to have fun, so I didn't expect things to be anything but drudgery. Gram's invitation brought a second illumination: she wouldn't have said those words unless she believed more was possible for me.

She wouldn't have suggested that I pursue something unattainable. As a New Englander, as a product of Depression-era sensibility, she was a pragmatic woman. Compared to me these days, she was far less likely to say fanciful or frivolous things. More than anything, she was a loving and caring grandmother. She believed in me! If she believed I could enjoy my life, I could believe it, too.

After reading the book *The Art of Possibility*, I borrowed Benjamin Zander's words and claimed the idea that Gram had created not an expectation for me to live up to, but a possibility for me to live into. A possibility that I deeply desired to live into.

It's funny but I really did have to believe that enjoying life was a real thing. I had spent my life viewing "happy people" with envy, but also with intense skepticism. Could this be real? Is there such a thing as living without constant angst, anxiety, and discomfort? I vacillated between thinking they must be lying, and lamenting that they had been given access to something I hadn't.

I asked myself the question, what would make my life more enjoyable? What immediately flashed into my mind were all the deficits I described in my introduction: I wanted to be healthier, I wanted a greater sense of community, I wanted greater confidence to pursue opportunities, especially work-and-career related ones.

Doors started to open as I leaned into believing in possibility, believing in magic, believing in miracles. I began to take care of my health, but with a whole new energy, and a strong sense of inner authority. It wasn't about a nebulous new set of rules about what was supposedly healthy or good for me. I began to focus on feeling good, feeling capable and in control. I began to focus on what would help me enjoy my life and it empowered me. These feelings were new and yet oddly familiar. It was the way I'd wanted to feel all my life. It felt like who I was designed to be.

The more I practiced my new habits, the more radiantly healthy and strong I felt, which expanded my sense of what my life could become. My physical flexibility increased and with it, my cognitive and even emotional flexibility. It made me wonder just how much more was possible for me.

If I can start to enjoy today, what will tomorrow be like? What else can shift? Who else can I become? What can God do in my life if I listen to Him, respond to Him?

Daring to dream often feels the biggest risk of them all. If we reveal to others what we dream of, they can be let down when we don't achieve it. Or they can laugh at or mock us (whether to our faces or not) for even dreaming it at all. Fear of this kind of humiliation can create a block to even dreaming our dreams in private, from letting them flourish and grow. It can feel like a sound strategy to simply settle. This is how dreams become buried.

I'm fascinated by the subject of long-buried dreams and how to excavate them. I believe many people have buried old dreams and I love to discuss what they are, how they became covered, and what can be done to start to dig. There is a kernel of what God has placed on my heart as a dream that has to do with this very subject, and I'm still waiting for the details to be revealed.

Resurrected Dreams

Right now, the dream I'm called to pursue is about writing this book. I've gotten a taste of what it's like to impact others with my story, to open their eyes to possibility, to participate in that process. I am dreaming of that on a much wider scale. I'm dreaming about readers feeling endeared toward my sweet grandmother and her living legacy.

As my faith journey unfolds, I learn to trust God's timing. I dreamed of being a writer since childhood, writing stories when I was 10, 11, 12. I was praised for my writing in high school, which inspired fantasies in my college years. I majored in English. I mailed short stories off to literary magazines found in the annual Publisher's Guide. In return, I received neatly-typed rejection letters, relatively few compared to what some great writers tout, but enough to make me believe it wasn't meant to be. I felt frustrated and resentful. I kicked sand over that dream and moved on to pursue other things that seemed more...well.... possible.

I changed my goal from writing to teaching, which appeared more practical and, I suppose, more noble. I was hung up on doing something that would prove I was worthy to take up space and breathe clean air. I was stuck on the idea that I had to earn my worthiness with good works. All of this untruth has fallen away now but it was powerfully at play in my choices back then.

Goals around teaching became pursuit of a few kinds of counseling: career and academic advising, mental health counseling, family therapy. I kept giving more, sacrificing more, trying to earn the favor of the world. The faster I ran, the more lost I became, like someone running into the woods as darkness gathers at nightfall. Eventually, I found myself panting and exhausted, no idea how I'd ended up in this mire, unsure of which way to go or if it was even worth continuing to try.

I've carried a lot of shame about my career dead ends. As a former honor student, I clung desperately to a narrative my teachers had spoken about my potential. With each stumble, I branded myself a bigger failure. In the past, I blamed myself for squandering my opportunities, but I now see it differently. I see the lessons that came from these experiences, each teaching me to understand my own strengths and limitations.

Most of all, my twisting and winding path through the world of work taught me to fully rely on God, the One who designed and created me, who knows better than I do how I should use my gifts in the world. It took a long time, but as I've turned to Him, I've been shown clearly which opportunities to step into and how to use them for my own good and His glory.

I have some favorite praise songs that reference "resurrecting dreams" and the phrase is starting to replace "excavating dreams" in the way I speak. So much of what has broken people's hearts and spirits has to do with losing their way in pursuit of their heartfelt dreams. It's often the world that led them astray, but God takes the fall. Still, I'm electrified by the image of Jesus touching these fading dreams with his resurrection power and bringing them back into vivid life and new possibilities.

My resurrected dream IS related to my original dream; it has to do with being creative and writing and learning about unique ways people do their work and live out their unique purposes. It ties back to career counseling in some way that's not yet been revealed. But I also pray and submit myself to be of use in the Kingdom of Heaven's work here on Earth. I want to serve God in whatever way He would have me serve. I can't even guess what shape or form that will take as the remaining years of my life become decades. The future is unknowable to me but fully known by God and there is freedom in that.

On Your Doorstep

In the midst of the messy, emotional process of cleaning out Gram's house, I found so many small, seemingly random things. Some I claimed as possessions and others I claimed simply as signs. One that fit both categories was a slip of paper on which was written, in Gram's tight, old-school cursive: *Every morning is a miracle left on your doorstep by God.*

There's no way to know for sure when she wrote it down or even why, but I suspect she heard someone say it (maybe on TV) and carefully transcribed it onto the paper, which she stuck in a book until the day I was to find it. Just like Enjoy Your Life, it has become something that guides and grows my expansive sense of possibility. I kept the slip of paper and I still have it taped inside a decorative box that made the cut when we down-sized.

Another little treasure was a morning prayer on a yellowing square of what we always called "oak tag" - it was held to her refrigerator by a magnet for most of the years in my memory. It's full of little gems about approaching tasks cheerfully and suffering fools gladly. While I don't recite the prayer word for word every day, the spirit of it is with me. It reminds me that all things are possible when we walk in continuous spiritual harmony with God. It's a way to stay connected to Him and to Gram to surrender my own desires and submit my will, again and again, each morning.

I try to approach each day with the energy that it is a miracle waiting to happen. I wear my Mantraband bracelet that says "Expect Miracles." I surrender to the Holy Spirit my closed-minded and negative thinking, and any limits I may create in the day because of a tendency to rely on myself. I ask the Holy Spirit to enter the equation and bring into my path all the things I need. I also ask for specifics, such as wanting my writing to touch people's hearts and for my books to sell so that I can keep writing them. I ask boldly and I receive.

It is never too late to believe in possibility. You are never too old to pursue a long-buried dream, or to pray to have that dream resurrected. If God placed it on your heart, He is waiting for you to turn toward Him for the courage to begin again. He already has the guidance for where you should go next. He's waiting for you. It's your move.

As new possibilities bloom, it becomes impossible not to Enjoy Your Life.

CHAPTER 5

Participation

Act, Move, Get Uncomfortable.

ENJOY YOUR LIFE invited me into active participation with the Holy Spirit. As I continued my Enjoy-Your-Life Pursuit, it became clear that I was going to have to do things I'd never done.

If I wanted everything I could see in my dreams, I had to act. If I truly desired all that had been placed on my heart, I had to act. I had to move. I had to work. I had to do things that might not be instantly comfortable.

Each human effort is made in the presence of God, in His attention and with His care, so we can operate in a continuous, unbreakable loop of support and feedback through His Spirit. We can ask Him what to do and how to do it; He can show us how well we are doing. Our lives are a dynamic, co-creative process. This truth thrills me every time I soak it in.

When I first began to feel this, to witness it at work in my circumstances, it created a crackle of excitement like none I'd ever experienced. There is an account on Instagram that makes me chuckle; it's called @godcaresbro. But my invitation into participation was a little bit like a lightbulb going off: WOW! God cares, bro! God knows, cares, and wants to be involved with me. God has been waiting for me so we could get going!

I began to understand that a huge component in creating and maintaining my Mire was ducking out, hiding, not showing up for my life. I understand that I did this initially for self-protective reasons. It's normal for children to find ways to stay safe. As time went on, resentment became intoxicating and the Mire became inescapable. It was powerfully driven by my desire to avoid further crushing disappointment. It just hurt too much.

And yet, as with the paradox inherent in so many of our human ways, there was a layer beneath, one that DID want the disappointment. Like poking a toothache, I listened to the dark voices that said, see, failure is evidence. The disappointment supplied proof that I should stay safely tucked in my Mire. Another repeating loop.

I had jobs where I performed well enough on the surface, but I was so unhappy, uncomfortable, and anxious behind the scenes that I could only cope outside of work by numbing, mostly by overeating. There were also lots of jobs I ran after, believing they were ideal for me, and I poured myself into cover letters, resumes, and serial job interviews, only to be told No. Every dead end proved joy was not meant for me.

When things were at their worst, I numbed with both food and alcohol. I didn't want to feel anything. Even as those real compulsions ran rampant, my addiction to negative thoughts did the most damage. Numbing behaviors increased as a way to quiet the thoughts.

As a person meeting every criteria on checklists for Highly Sensitive status, it hurt me to be rejected, to be passed over, to feel cast onto the reject pile. As this happened over and over, I retreated into the Mire where life was predictably sad but safe. I checked out. I figured I couldn't be disappointed when I didn't expect anything.

The moment of my grandmother's death arrived when I'd stopped showing up in every possible way. I had resigned from my final job as a mental health counselor AND voluntarily relinquished my license to practice. Knowing how little I had to give, it felt like the safest route, beating life at the punch. I quit before I could be fired, admitted failure before anyone had accused it. I burned with hot shame on the inside, but for the sake of my family, I muttered feeble excuses and fumbled to find the next thing.

That thing was teaching courses at the local community college and while it brought some satisfaction, even connections with students that persist to this day, I was out of my element. I didn't understand the concept of spiritual participation or how to ask for help. Each challenge felt fraught with risk, my fear of failure at an all-time high.

I was not looking within; I was not accessing the spiritual support that was as close as my breath. I accepted all the responsibility AND all the blame for what felt like a fumbling, pathetic series of events in my life, ashamed to seek God with such an embarrassing mess.

I picked up freelance transcription work to supplement the meager pay from teaching adjunct courses. The typing was mostly uninspired but at least it was operating in my zone of competence. Of course, paying the bills and feeding our kids were pressing concerns, regardless of how discouraged I felt about my career path. Like teaching, transcription had its small satisfactions, that moment you've turned a complicated audio file into a clean transcript, but there was no sense in it of co-creating with the Spirit. There was no fresh wind, no energy of inspiration.

In the months before my grandmother passed, my days blurred one into the next. I herded my kids from bed to school, then pounded down sugar and caffeine to come alive, or at least function. While working from home in pajamas can be joyful for some, it wasn't for me. Just like the years when I had stayed home with my toddlers, it felt by default, not decision. It felt like it was happening to me. I felt isolated, restless, and bored. I felt heavy, sluggish, and like life had passed me by. I felt mired.

Later, as I began to shift into my physical transformation, I asked the question, if I am to enjoy my life, what should I be doing with my work? How should I use my gifts and talents? How can I feel intellectually stimulated? How should I make a contribution to the world?

Prophets of an Unknown Future

These questions led me to apply to work as a medical scribe for a busy surgeon. The role was brand new, a formal job description barely inked, a training program non-existent. In many ways, based on my Masters level education and past professional experiences, I was overqualified. However, from the moment I learned of it, I felt....called. Called into participation. My ongoing pursuit of Enjoy Your Life tuned me in to receive this calling.

I look back at the decision to apply to be a scribe and my four years in that role as the most life-changing of my entire existence. Working in a hospital setting, becoming intimately acquainted with patients who were sick and dying, watching my mentor surgeon tenderly care for people, it changed me. It made me understand that we are in active participation with Spirit, with God, in a moment-to-moment way if we choose to access that. We can ask for support, be guided, and get confirmation of the correctness of our steps.

I watched Dr. Starks doing God's work here on the earth, comforting and healing with his hands. I remember learning that he prayed immediately before entering the operating room. As the patient was being prepared, he was preparing himself, and I was deeply inspired by that acknowledgement of participation. Though I knew I hadn't been called to become a surgeon, here I was, part of a surgeon's healing work in the world. One day, as a way of praising my work, Dr. Starks gave me a copy of a prayer called "Prophets of an Unknown Future." The prayer makes it clear that all efforts, no matter how small, are vital to the Kingdom of Heaven's work on Earth.

Those days felt anointed. I felt so seen. It was like God whispering into my ear, "You are special and you are called to help do My will in the world." That crackle of participation-electricity intensified in me. I started to approach every day with conviction and excitement like I'd never felt before.

I've been asked the question, how do you "know" it was God, that spark of motivation to step out and apply for a job that made little sense? I give the answer that Joan of Arc is purported to have responded to an interrogator at her tribunal, "How else would God speak to me if not through my imagination?" I felt it in my bones, in my soul.

It was a visceral, gut-level assuredness that this was God getting my attention, God working in me and through me. I remember standing in the hallway outside Dr. Starks' office, getting ready to go see the next patient, suffused with the joy of serving in a unique, special way. I thought, wow, all of my prayers were heard all along! God knew I needed this kind of work! God saw me and well, He cares, bro!

Though I'd been raised in 80s Catholicism with the sacraments of First Eucharist, Reconciliation and Confirmation, I stopped attending Mass around age 14 or 15. Like her mother before her, my mother was a devoted attendant of Mass for much of her life, but had a disagreement with our parish priest and stopped attending when I was a teenager. Though she found a new church, it was a confusing and hurtful experience for the family, and it happened at a time when I wanted to leave "it" all behind anyway.

I didn't get that walking away from the Catholic Church wasn't the same thing as walking away from God altogether. I wanted to toss all of it away, feeling spurned, sensing no enduring tie.

I'd been taught rote, memorized prayers, and while I see beauty in the meditative ritual of the Rosary, praying didn't connect as a genuine conversation with God back then. I still make the sign of the Cross any time I pass an accident scene. I acknowledge that rituals of Catholicism are also part of my spiritual DNA.

I did pray in my own way. I formed earnest, if clumsy, prayers throughout my 20s and 30s. I prayed from inside the Mire, and I know those prayers were heard, but at the time my faith was shaky. Back then, prayer was not my go-to; it was not the natural, intuitive practice that it is for me now. It felt a little more like tossing a coin into a wishing well rather than a bold certainty than my words were heard and would garner a response, even if not the one I wanted.

It was in my grandmother's death and my plea to understand how to move forward in grief that brought my prayer life front and center. I have never been the same. Now I go to prayer instantly, instinctively. If intercession is desperately needed, I go to my knees without even thinking about it.

Working as a scribe came about because I prayerfully sought next steps and was directed to an opportunity to show up and participate. The job brought needed energy to my days. It reinvigorated my intellectual curiosity. Suddenly I had a reason to refresh my medical terminology, left mostly by the wayside since the kids were babies. I had a cause to learn about new diseases, the latest clinical research, and the entire process of working up a patient from start to finish.

I wasn't a medical student, but Dr. Starks treated me with respect as though I was. He taught me to understand his diagnostic process so I could quickly and accurately scribe his notes. I sensed his admiration and soaked up his approval. It was another important part of my unmiring to feel seen and acknowledged not just by God but by a fellow human being who I held in high regard.

The days became weeks, then months. My previously fast typing sped up even further, my fingers flying across the keyboard. We streamlined the workflow in preparing charts to be ready for a patient's visit. I felt such a strong sense of participation in the care of people who were distressed, confused by their diagnosis. God was showing me clearly that He saw my desire to be put to use during those frustrating years. How wonderful it was to see that my clumsy prayers had been answered after all.

This job and the ways it was challenging me, bringing my intellectual curiosity back into the forefront, fueling my sense of capability, it brought genuine revelation. Knowing I was in moment-to-moment participation with Spirit changed how I approached my work. So did the idea that I'd been hand selected by God and guided to it. Suddenly, the girl who previously had trouble dragging herself out of bed couldn't wait to get up in the morning.

Everything started to sparkle for me the way I'd seen it sparkling for others while I was still inside the Mire. I felt a kind of enthusiasm I'd never known before. I couldn't wait to get up to the hospital each day. I looked forward to the following Monday morning as I was walking out to head home on Friday afternoon. I loved my job!

It isn't that I wasn't enjoying the non-work parts of my life that occurred in the places & spaces between my work days. I was enjoying all of my life! I loved and appreciated life outside work all the more for the contrast it created. My self care, my fasting and feasting, all of it was enhanced because I saw it as a means to support my work and participation with Spirit.

Eventually, the desire to participate began to shift everything in my spiritual life. As I prayed, I was answered with messages about what to do. The answers started as a compelling desire to move my body, to propel the temple of my spirit forward. Daily digestive rest and great nutrition were increasing my energy level, so I began to walk as much as possible, to feel the flow of encountering new spaces, wide-eyed with wonder.

After lunch, I'd stand quietly on the sidelines of an exam room doing my scribe work, but I was becoming increasingly restless in both body and spirit. It was as though God was urging me to be available and alert for the Holy Spirit encounters that would plant the next seeds.

The Unbelievable Freedom Era

As months passed, the urging morphed into a desire to be more visible and vocal. After years of dutifully documenting in the background, I wanted to use my voice. I had something to say and I was growing in confidence to say it. The feeling took root that yes, this transformation happening inside me was worth talking about and worth sharing. I increased the amount that I was showing up online, crafting posts on my personal social media accounts and eventually on a blog. We started to draft what became the first book *Unbelievable Freedom*. It was the birth of my career as a writer.

The first book accomplished more than we'd imagined it could, both of us being first time authors. We garnered thousands of sales and hundreds of reviews from around the world. We built an online community of fans and followers. Somewhere along the way, we became "the Super Shrinking Smiths" and enjoyed our 15 minutes of fame, a relative thing these days, but fun nonetheless.

When I reflect on myself at the height of that phase, it makes me shake my head. I'd gone from fully mired to basking in my long-sought idea of happiness. Dreams were coming true and I was pinching myself. I thought it might be as good as things could ever get, but I still had a lot to learn.

The specific decision to share my weight loss publicly is a concrete example of my willingness to participate with Spirit and be led to those who wanted/needed help. Over and over, as I shared my journey through my writing, I received confirmation from people who said, "Your story gave me hope, the way you expressed it encouraged me, now I feel inspired to make a change." At the heart of these messages was: You make me believe I can enjoy life. By passing on the permission that my grandmother had given to me, I was participating with Gram and with the Holy Spirit, too.

I'm humbled by the sheer number of people who have said to me, "I love your writing." Did I not pray to hear that? Is that not, in itself, evidence that dreams come true and that the desires of our hearts are meant to come into existence? It all depends on one's beliefs and current place in their faith journey. For me, it's exciting to walk this path and watch my faith bear ripe fruit.

Moving into action, receiving confirmation, then acting again, it created a powerful participation loop that's still in motion as I type these words. It has created all that's happened in the venture we call Unbelievable Freedom LLC. It led to my podcast. It led to the series of workbooks I curated with several collaborating authors. Each subsequent project that shares my story or someone's else's is motivated by a desire to stay in participation and out of the mire.

Participation came to mean so much more than just a frame for work. It began to prompt my engagement in life itself. I'd previously clung to the idea that I was socially anxious and avoidant, but I now see this was another excuse to maintain the mire. Claiming anxiety was self protection against my fear, but I didn't need it any longer. As I felt the Spirit stirring in me each day, I wanted to take part in ALL things. I got more interested in family gatherings and social outings. I made new friends. I danced. I sang karaoke.

Seeing God's hand everywhere, in everything, made ME want to be everywhere, in everything. I had an urge to travel, and I followed it, criss-crossing the United States and even taking a tropical cruise. Each trip I took felt like one more way to discover God and myself in a new setting and I loved it. I experienced pure delight at being out in the world, moving, seeing, feeling, using all my senses. I referred to my daily pursuit as "Collecting Easy Delights" and this became part of what I called my intentional contentment practice, my Poster Girl Habits. I replaced worry with worship and suddenly I was participating in pure magic.

As I sit here typing these words, wondering who you are, the future readers of this unfinished book, I'm making a very clear plea to God. I ask that He allow me to participate in His work. I'm a sort of 'prophet of a future not yet known', and I ask daily to participate. I want others to feel the freedom I believe is our design and our birthright.

I have no ability on my own to bring others to freedom. Only God can do that - and He will! He has done it before and He will do it again. Everything He has done to restore me to my original design - to make me more like Him - THIS is who He is and what He does. He's still in the business of redeeming lives and there's nothing more thrilling than that.

So whether from here, I become a writer in an even more real sense, signing contracts and earning money to create more books in the future, or whether I return to being a scribe.... whether I go back to working in education or social services, or do something entirely new, Enjoy Your Life is what taught me about participation. It taught me to be bold, not timid, and to move with trust instead of trepidation.

Participation will be a key ingredient in the development of your Enjoy Your Life formula, too.

CHAPTER 6

Praise

A Door Flung Wide

ENJOY YOUR LIFE creates a deep desire to give praise for, well, the enjoyment!

There is an upwelling of such deep gratitude that it is nearly overwhelming. I love the lyric that says praise is an open door to an open Heaven. It has been just that for me, a wide, welcoming invitation into bliss.

Part of the treasure hunt that has been my Enjoy-Your-Life Pursuit is to really deconstruct the meaning of those three words. This is where I really wanted to use a secret decoder ring, which I now understand as asking the Holy Spirit for support. I'm focused on the JOY part of Enjoy and I use it way more in casual conversation, "Enjoy your coffee!" And "Enjoy the movie!" Etc.

I've also looked at what the word joy really means. Whether I was right or wrong, I had a sense growing up that my mom and dad were leading joyless lives. If they felt joy, I didn't feel it from them. I'm not blaming them, and I expect they had their own mires to work through. But it left me with a lot of questions about what joy means, and whether it is real.

Research and reading are central to how I learn, but my understanding of joy is totally experiential. As I have drawn closer to

God, I've experienced a joy that expands to fill me and overflow from me. Often, it makes me weep because it's so powerful, overwhelming in the best way. This is what makes Psalm 16's variations of "In His presence is fullness of joy" so meaningful. Enjoy Your Life means for me, being in His presence and being in a state of joy. I now do all things that will strengthen and maintain connection to that presence.

Joy is my health plan. Joy is my beauty plan. Joy is how I interrupt anxiety. Joy is how I manage both my internal life and my external one. Because I am joyful, I am able to be truly grateful.

During my time in the mire, I understood the importance of gratitude. I probably read about it! I adopted an 'attitude of gratitude' and practiced expressing it, but understood the neat and tidy kind listed in a cute gratitude journal. There's certainly nothing wrong with a list of thank you's for grandmothers, butterflies, birds, good cups of coffee, hot bowls of soup, flowers in a vase, alllllll the awesome things.

BUT over time, my engagement with that kind of gratitude weakened because it needed a reverberation. My thankfulness was just being sent up and out into....nothing. I came to need this praise to have a real recipient. And once I did, the gratitude was anything but tidy. It's messy and it's wild like a rushing river. My overflowing gratitude for being vibrantly alive, lifted out of the mire, brought back to life, it all needed to be sent out and received back again in a continual, reverberating flow. This joy is exactly what my relationship with Jesus has brought to me. I love Jesus and He loves me back.

How can I even begin to describe how I feel about praising the Lord? I was born to do it and frankly, I want to do it as my full-time occupation. To an extent, I do. I've fashioned my life to be on permanent spiritual retreat. The decision that I've made to "come out" and speak publicly about my love for God and my desire to follow Jesus is exactly that. It's an effort to craft something holistic where my work is to stay in an elevated state of praise as much as I can.

I need to say something here about praise music, traditional hymns but even more, a wide variety of contemporary gospel and praise songs. Prior to moving into my current spiritual alignment, I could not stand any of that music. I probably used the words that I "hated" it. It felt irritating at best and triggering at worst. It felt like a reminder of all the people who were in some kind of exclusive club with God while I just could not find my way inside. It annoyed me. It fed my resentment.

Because of the time I now spend listening to the very same music, because of the way God uses it to speak directly into my heart and soul, I understand the mechanism from its flip side. This kind of music is such a powerful tool. It enlists praise as a true spiritual weapon, so it will be resisted until it can't be resisted any more. The same goes for other praise-related practices. When God is working hardest to draw someone in, this sort of thing becomes intolerable until it is irresistible. His ways are mysterious indeed.

Praise is a spiritual coping skill for me now. Praise is an interrupter; it's a way to break free from struggle when it's attempting to take hold. You cannot worship and worry; you cannot praise and despair. This is a phenomenon I know so deeply that I can't unknow it.

Praise is far more than just speaking or singing. It's an invitation for the Holy Spirit to enter your atmosphere, to come into the room, whatever your space may be. I ask for a fresh wind to blow in. I ask the Spirit to hover close, to descend on me, fill me up, to amplify every part of me that feels powerful and to accommodate for those that don't. I have never vibrated at a frequency higher than that of pure praise. It is transcendent, electric, other-wordly.

I often weep when I'm in a state of intense praise. I've always cried easily and I'm not particularly ashamed to do so in regular contexts. But my tears of praise, I've come to understand, are anointed by the Holy Spirit. When I have been in periods of deep healing, I will praise and weep and the tears are cleansing me, washing away all remnants of my old nature, making me new, refining me. Man, it's beautiful!

Anyone who knows about what's been going on with my spiritual life, especially the past year or two, knows I talk about "walking around in the woods and crying." This is what I'm referring to. Getting out in nature, being close to God, communing with Him and feeling my wounds healing. It makes me weep for relief, satisfaction, and joy.

Intimate + Ecstatic

If you watch contemporary praise music videos, especially ones that involve spontaneous worship, you'll hear many invitations from those speaking and singing. They invite the Holy Spirit to enter, to fill the room, to stay close by. Even watching these videos from my own home (or a coffeehouse, or a public park) I can feel the Spirit moving in those rooms. The intimacy of the experience takes my breath. And I love watching the truth of it in the faces and movements of the people present. I know how they feel!

They feel INTIMACY because of the peace and contentment of being seen, known, accepted, loved, saved forever. The exposure of laying it all down in praise makes any other kind of vulnerability pale in comparison. It's being stripped bare and fully revealed before God with nothing hidden. It is finally understanding we've always been seen and always been loved. Our false selves or egos of this world are poured out and the Spirit refills the space that remains.

They feel ECSTASY because of the joy of alignment with truth, with original design, being the image of God, being forever connected to Him and destined for Heaven. This kind of deep thankfulness, the intense relief it brings... it is, well, ecstatic! We were designed and built to praise in this way.

I believe that the intimacy and ecstasy of complete surrender in praise is the best way we can understand from here on earth a bit of how Heaven will feel, more of the streaks that shone in my grandparents' front room.

The lyrics of a song called "Thank You" by Maverick City Music capture the intimacy + ecstasy of my gratitude for seeing truth:

You sang 'til I found my song
You danced 'til my heart woke up
Now I move to the rhythm of love
I can't praise You enough
You wept 'til I found my strength
You lost your breath dying to save me
Now I'll never go back to that grave
I can't praise You enough

If the mundane things we do as human people to serve in this world is participation with the Holy Spirit, praise is an elevation of that energy. Praise feels like fire in my heart, like these lyrics from "The Wick" by Housefires:

Oooh my heart is the wick
Your love is the flame
And I wanna burn for your name

I love praising God more than anything I've ever loved. It is "my thing" like some people love dance and some love animals and some bake, paint, garden. I know it is what I was born to do, what I was hard-wired for. It feels like joy. It feels like truth. It feels like freedom.

Praise feels like me in my flannel nightie on a register in my grandmother's front room, warm and safe, confident in the abundance of the love I receive. It feels like a thirsty person drinking from an overflowing well. Jesus is a well that never runs dry.

I claimed "Praise" as my word for 2021, and while choosing a thematic word is part of secular self-improvement-ism, the decision was a deeply holy offering. Praise is what I claim as my word and my offering forever.

I don't know what your personal way of praising God might look like, but I have a strong sense of what it can feel like. It is worth being vulnerable, worth the risk of doing something new and unfamiliar, to pursue this high vibration of truth.

Experiment with praise. Surrender to joy. Enjoy Your Life.

CHAPTER 7

Pruning

Gardens Require Tending

ENJOY YOUR LIFE requires constant pruning and God is the gardener. I adore the image of God as a vine keeper, trimming and cutting, pruning and pampering. This too is a participative process. I can see my spiritual life for a long time as a garden, one that never died but became overgrown with weeds because I neglected to participate.

It's interesting to contemplate the interplay of the pruning and the surrendering. God has given us all a free will, so those things he is pruning away, I'm also surrendering, because even as he takes things out of my life, it's my decision to let them go, refraining from stewing, ruminating, and looking backwards. Some days are better than others on this note.

Now that I have finally put God first in my life, He shows me the areas of my life where I should invest my effort and energy. I see other pieces that should be allowed to fall away and I work to be obedient. I claim my status as an unfinished masterpiece, constantly being sculpted and improved, like a mature garden that gets better with tending and time.

I love the imagery of a refining fire through the Holy Spirit, as illustrated by the lyric printed in the opening of this book. I love that God always saw the beauty under my tarnish. I receive the idea of being purified as I am pruned, all of my old sin nature being burned up, revealing the pure truth of my original design.

Anyone who knows me (or who has seen the cover of this book!) won't be surprised to hear that I love flowers. My first memories of flowers are connected to my grandmother. She had flower beds full of annuals and perennials. I specifically recall lily of the valley. In my own adult life, I had purple crocus that pushed their way up through snow banks in early spring, stubborn and resilient. Seeing them each year after Gram died reminded me of her words, planted long before her death, and how they continued to grow in my life.

I've also written in a few places about orchids, those delicate beauties that only thrive in very specific conditions. There's a "orchid and dandelion" theory about sensitive children that has always hit home with me. When I look at my struggle, I recognize that I needed a very particular kind of environment to thrive and I didn't always get enough of those features. But God was always with me, and was consistently at work through people like my grandmother, who watered and sheltered me just enough that I persevered.

Gram also loved hummingbirds. In my teens, I bought her a series of decorative plates with different hummingbird breeds hovering near various flowers. After she died, I couldn't bear to part with them, so I wrapped and packed them away until we were downsizing to move to our current apartment.

That's when I discovered that several were broken and glued back together. Some had clearly broken more than once. She'd had them on a particular shelf and now that I think about it, balanced in their little wire stands, they would have been at risk of falling and smashing as people slammed out the side door of her house (as we were all prone to do.)

I was deeply moved by the picture of my tiny grandmother super-gluing the delicate shards back together. She cherished the plates because I had given them to her and because she cherished me, plus she was a frugal New Englander who didn't throw things away. But it remains true that through her love and support, God has put my broken pieces back together many times. Now that I am whole, he can set about stripping away all that's not of Him.

In addition to all that my pursuit of Enjoy Your Life has given and gifted me, it has taken many things away. This is also part of His divine pruning. This image is not mine and not unique, but it resonates. I read the quote, "In the pruning, you will meet the Gardener like never before." This is my truth. It's what this most recent chapter of my life has been about. I have never been closer to God and the closer I get, the closer I want to be. Fully known is a phrase that resonates.

The most significant pruning that God accomplished in my life was the stripping away of my unbelief. I'm asked if I've always believed in God, and while the answer is essentially yes, that faith was wobbly and half-hearted for much of my life. Believing in God seemed like an optional accessory rather than an absolute necessity. I made the decision to keep my belief in a box on a shelf, but eventually, Jesus busted out of that box the way He busted out of the grave at the resurrection. As He did, my residual unbelief was cut away and cast out.

I began to surrender my unbelief after my grandmother died and I prayed in earnest to believe. God answered those prayers in a mighty way. To support that growth, he freed me from many old compulsions or "addictions." Some of them were more simple and straightforward like my habits around processed starches and sugars, and the damage that my old way of eating was doing to my health. Others are more complex, like my habits with my thinking, my internal narrative around struggle, and even my identity as someone meant to be resentful and bitter. Good riddance! Praise the Lord!

These are things I must surrender over and over. They have not been pruned away with a tidy lopping off like an actual limb from a tree. I have to recognize them as not of God, not part of who He designed me to be, and choose to let them go. As I earnestly release my grip on them and ask that they be lifted from me, they are removed. This doesn't mean they're gone forever. They can and will creep back in. I will talk about this more in the next section on Pitfalls.

Before I do, I want to say a bit about the things I've surrendered in terms of circumstances. While I can't claim zero reluctance, when prayer has shown me God wants me to move away from something, I have done it. I have been willing to give up: friendships with people not aligned with my journey, a job with glimmers of promise of growth for the future, owning a home, living in a city where I grew up and had connections.

In the midst of this transformation, I experienced what I thought was a nudge from God about selling real estate. I'd been following curiosity, as Elizabeth Gilbert calls it, studying the architecture of houses and buildings around our city. I'd become interested in the way people decorate their homes and arrange them to suit their family and their lifestyle. It seemed a logical next step to get involved in the industry, so I studied for a sales agent license, and spent two years working to establish a local reputation, working with a few buyers and sellers along the way.

And then my prayers started focusing on how to grow in real estate and become one of the people I saw getting accolades, making great money. But the answer that came again and again was this: don't. Don't grow in real estate; don't seek status or success in this area. Do not continue spending energy on how to grow your skills or connections there. That's not what I have for you. It felt very much like my departure from my role as a medical scribe. It came down to my will or God's, so I followed His directive. My peers from my old real estate team are achieving amazing things in a hot market, and I'm reminded to trust what God is actively doing right now.

He has also pruned away all the "wrong" or misaligned parts of what I have done with Unbelievable Freedom as a platform. It definitely began as a platform focused on one couple's weight loss story and spent a period of time with that at its heart: physical wellness, food and nutrition, and trappings that come with all that. We are living in a world full of micro-influencers with small rooftops from which they can shout out their personal message. I was one of millions. While this didn't have to be a terrible thing, it was a noisy and confusing place for me.

It began to fuel a kind of pride that was purely of this world and what it values. It was about taking photos in the right clothes, posed at the right angles. I repeatedly wrestled with the way the pictures made me feel proud, followed by the reminder from God that His plans and purpose for me are so far above a fancy dress or a pair of jeans.

Although my weight loss story is an important part of my testimony, showing up as a weight loss influencer became another trap, one leading me back toward The Mire. Feeling obsessed with being "thin" or getting "thinner" for its own sake is another way to walk apart from God, to be self-focused and self-glorified and overly identified with struggle. This took time for me to recognize, but once I did, it weighed on me (pun intended) until I spoke my truth.

Each time I showed up in a weight loss focused group, including the one that I had stepped up to lead, I would feel a shift from enjoying my life into struggle. I saw so many women at a healthy weight yet obsessively focused on losing just 5 or 10 more pounds. It was like they were marinating in struggle energy, and it was way too familiar. It was aligning me with people still deep within their own mires. While it's possible that my boundaries needed strengthening, something had to change. I knew it wasn't my place to judge them but it WAS my place to recognize the misalignment and surrender.

Maybe I just got confused by the attention that my weight loss success brought to me. Of course, I wanted to be considered a success. I'd spent years being ambivalent about being looked at, but the bigger part of that was a desire to be truly seen. I had a lifelong desire for confirmation that I was special and worthy of accolades. Suddenly, seemingly, there they were! Even as I chose to share photos of the weight falling off, something else felt off.

What I deeply desired was to be truly seen and fully known. Only God could give this to me, but I did not see what was happening. I would put up a comparison collage in an online group, seeing for myself the brightened light in my eyes, the heaviness that had lifted from my spirit, but comments would focus on asking about the tags in my clothing or what I was eating for dinner. I was so frustrated! Couldn't they see me? Couldn't they see how much I was doing the inner work? Couldn't they see my freedom? I spun my wheels. The Mire beckoned.

I was still seeking the world's approval and that was the wrong course. I haven't talked much about people-pleasing behavior, and there are a number of reasons why. It's a broad and vague topic that encompasses so many behaviors, and most people get caught up in it to some degree or another. We are wired to want love and acceptance and that's easily twisted into a desire for approval.

For me, what's been helpful is the concept of Fight-Flight-Freeze-Fawn. The fourth trauma response, fawning, became a comfortable way for me to avoid conflict and generally hide. Whether for approval or self protection or both, throughout my life, I've fawned by pretending to agree with people when in my heart, I disagree. I have tried to morph and mold myself into what I think they want me to be. I have tried to smile and get along.

Some of my relationships with the online weight loss community were becoming about fawning, a self-repressive desire to just be approved of, no matter what it took, I knew it needed to be pruned away. There is something about coming to resonate with the resurrection, to feel the victory of Jesus as a personal triumph, that emboldens us. It casts out timidity and makes it impossible to behave in ways that are essentially lies. I started to see how wrong it was to repress my real self as God had designed me to think, feel, and be. I felt old, timid, fawning me being pruned.

I began to set strong boundaries with the folks from my old communities, and as I did, the "relationships" shriveled and dried up. There was genuine pain involved in letting some of them go. I will never forget walking in the forest, crying and hurting, but also praising God because I trusted Him and what He was pruning away from me. I knew then and now that it was for my good and His glory. I prayed God would show me a way to speak my actual truth and here I am, doing it.

I'm learning more about the way God has equipped us to wield spiritual weapons. As I've come to understanding fasting for *purely* spiritual reasons, to plan and devote a fast as a sacrifice, using the time to reflect and pray, I see the distinction clearly. Within a large weight loss community, there are many people who fast for no other reason than a worldly one. They want to be healthy or to become more slim and trim, and while health is important, this fasting was purely self-serving. I am not saying it's wrong, but just that I can recognize the difference. It's hollow to plan a fast for worldly reasons and simply claim "oh yeah, this is also a spiritual practice" when there is no genuine intent there.

Worse, sometimes the fasting and the way people approached it became a form of worship at the altar of suffering. Though I know the people in question could not see it, dieting was just their way to suffer for its own sake. Restricting food and feeling deprived becomes a form of bowing to another false idol. Because of my transformed attitude toward struggle, I don't want any part of that.

It took many months and a large sum of money, but after feeling the Holy Spirit urging me to do so, I applied for and secured a federal trademark for Unbelievable Freedom. Is this so that Unbelievable Freedom can be a big wellness/weight loss brand? I don't believe so. I feel God has anointed this platform and this brand for a much bigger purpose, and I'm waiting to see what that is. I only know that the next step is to tell my story in a more honest way, and that's what this book is for. God is fully redeeming the pain of losing my grandmother; He is turning it into the fuel that motivates me to participate with Him in this venture.

God has said through my prayers, I have given Unbelievable Freedom for you to steward. I want you to put all your energy into Unbelievable Freedom, into what you can do with books and content creation through this platform. He has spoken to me in my heart, in my imagination, just as Joan of Arc claimed at her tribunal. He has told me that Unbelievable Freedom is a platform to be used for His glory, something I can build and use to invite others into relationship with Him. The rest is yet to be revealed.

I don't know how things are going to look in the years to come. Although I love my family and am deeply grateful for my marriage and strong relationships with my adult children, this is a profoundly lonely time in my life. I spend much of my time alone in prayer and reflection. I do a lot of writing, but not a lot of interacting with others. I don't really have a community right now. While some of this is undoubtedly attributable to pandemic-related restrictions, I also accept that this may be God's plan for me right now.

Just a Dab Won't Do

I recognize that so many steps in this faith journey have been walked by others before me, and I find myself at familiar junctures, like the one where you start to wish you could somehow "go back" because while living in the world left me achingly empty, it made a certain sense. It made sense to my human brain and to most of the people around me. The loneliness comes from submitting to God every day, asking to see with eyes like His, but not encountering many others who seem to live the same way.

I certainly do have people in my midst who have beliefs that are aligned with mine. My friend Jen has been a spiritual mentor since childhood and her budding faith shone a light at dark times. I now call her my spiritual director and I'm a supporter of her growing effort to minister to others. The whole world is in a bit of a spiritual revival right now. Whether I go to a formal church in the future remains to be seen, but I suspect I will. I miss and desire the energy of people worshipping in community.

While I'm reading the Bible more closely, I'm cautious about the way many churches interpret the Bible or use it to instruct and direct others. I have received so much direct guidance from God and in equal measures, He's given me abundant, overflowing comfort. I don't want to disrupt that flow, so I proceed with mindful caution. I also walk with certainty that if God clearly shows me a church where He wants me to be, I am there.

I want to say a little bit here about New Age spirituality, something that has long fascinated me. In the many meandering years of my spiritual seeking, I was drawn to New Age philosophy like a moth to a flame. I went through phases of embracing 'woo woo', energy, and vibrations. I dabbled with the language of the Law of Attraction and attempted to explain the unexplainable appearance of blessings by saying I'd 'manifested' them with my thoughts, pulled them out of the 'field of possibility' with the magnetism of my mind. Hmmmmm, it always felt a little inauthentic to take credit for all this. I felt like a fraud boasting about blessings when I knew they should be ascribed to the same source that makes the sun rise and the oceans roar.

Though I never had the attention span to go far with any of it, I looked at astrology and the shifting of the planets. I even remember worrying once when I traveled during Mercury retrograde, when I should simply have been praying! I bought Tarot and other card decks, and I carried crystals in my pocket in hopes of attracting greater health and wealth. These things felt harmless for the most part. I called it all "high vibe" meaning, it was a way of focusing on how life is good and full of potential. I still agree with that, but the further I went, the more it was becoming one more road back to the mire.

While I'm on the topic, I want to say that secular self-improvement also called to me for a long time. It called out until it became another dead end in my search. Look at the words themselves, self-improvement; it purports to provide ways you can fix yourself. I reject that now as impossible. My belief is that without God, we will be locked in a cycle without access to the supernatural power needed for true restoration and redemption.

It was just like the way my weight loss journey, a bona fide success story with dramatic pictures and accolades from all directions, became a dissatisfying echo chamber. Yes, I'm a hard-working person who achieved a wonderful thing, and I do love myself. But the compliments started to make me prickle, as did all efforts at "self love" without God. It was self glorification and it was empty. God wasn't part of that broad public conversation and though it was my choice, it's one that triggered resentment until I changed my ways.

How can we really live from the power of our uniqueness without a Divine creator? How can we get enthusiastic about this narrative of being our own hero, the savior of our own story, no God required? I tried. I really did. I was led back to the living God again and again. And each time, I felt a deeper sense of relief and joy as I re-aligned with the truth.

I'm not here to denounce all New Age things as evil or ungodly. The strongest words I hear come out of my own mouth might be calling all of it "mumbo jumbo", which feels a little disrespectful toward what others endorse as belief, but it's how I feel. From the vantage point of the clarity I'm being given, it just feels like a whole lot of fluff.

I don't really understand what the Bible is saying about New Age things, and actually, I'm pretty tender on the whole subject of how to interpret the Bible. I'm brand new to approaching it as a tool for daily life.

I've read parts of the Bible over the years but I'm only right now, simultaneous to writing this book, reading the Bible cover to cover. That's a fair newbie by Bible reader standards. At times, I've thought of the Bible as a book weaponized to control people and at others, I've seen it as dusty and not particularly relevant to life in our day and age. The truth is that I was overwhelmed and unsure where to begin. Now that I'm responsive to the Holy Spirit, I'm reading and meditating on the Bible easily, and in this way, the Word is alive. Just as I was given new eyes to see situations in the world, I see the book in a new way when I read it through the lens of the Holy Spirit

Also, as a praying person, I'll say that God hasn't given me any specific directives to rid myself of the woo-woo (my card decks are still in a drawer; the crystals are still in a case on a shelf, etc).

But if I am going to tell the full story honestly, which I've attempted to do for this entire book, most of these items ring hollow for me. As I've wholeheartedly followed Jesus and surrendered to live in responsiveness to the Holy Spirit, these items stopped resonating as part of any spiritual practice. They were shiny and sparkly, but now they are dull. I'm not saying they can't be fun, but they've come to feel like playing when I want to do real work. They feel like dessert and spiritually, I want real food, real nourishment, real sustenance.

Here is a quote from the book of Job that sums up where my walk through New Age spirituality led me:

Such is the destiny of all who forget God; so perishes the hope of the godless. What they trust in is fragile ; what they rely on is a

spider's web. They lean on the web, but it gives way; they cling to it, but it does not hold (Job 8:13-15)

I cannot lean on a spider web when I've been shown clearly that there's a rock on which I can stand. I cannot trudge around in miry clay now that I have a firm foundation.

Still, it has been worth exploring how my mind works. I have always been one to observe others closely with a genuine desire to understand them. I believe it's part of the way I've been gifted. When I see people around me claim great freedom from a practice of pulling cards out of Tarot decks, I'm curious and sometimes even intrigued. I'm interested to know more about how that works and how it might possibly function for me in my quest. When I see others making decisions based on what the planets and stars do, and claiming to feel greater alignment in their lives, I want the same thing.

As I worked to move through the world following Jesus and being New Age-y, I found it constantly clashing. Clash, clash, clang. Every day, Spirit shakes my shoulders as I seek shiny so-called spiritual things.

Maybe others do it better, aligning these practices and the beliefs underneath them without a clash. For me, I tried hard in my writing and even in my personal conversations to substitute "The Universe" for God as a way of being inclusive to all. But the more I prayed, the more God encouraged me to say what I really feel and believe, which is that He reigns above it all, over the Universe and over everything.

When someone says love yourself, I hear: love God, in whose image I was made and whose Spirit lives within me. When someone says to raise my vibration, I turn to God's creation in nature and to praising Him through worship.

Another source of discord was the concept of "manifesting" - I'm totally comfortable describing the result of an answered prayer as a manifestation. That fits the dictionary definition, something theoretical being made real is to have manifested that thing. But in every conversation where manifesting was discussed without reference to God, I began to feel like something was missing. Just as effusive compliments on my weight loss felt like denying God the glory that is His, the same was the case with positive things occurring in my life.

As I feel more in tune with God through the Holy Spirit dwelling in me, I feel more known and seen, and I'm aware that this is the source of blessings and my answered prayers. I do not want to take credit for that which is His. Ever.

With the success of our first book, especially as sales racked up and we garnered a foreign rights deals, this came into play. I was congratulated with "Wow, you totally manifested that! You thought it right into existence!" But if I'm honest, even then I'd think, did I do that? Yes, I had faith and yes, I took inspired action, but I felt God's hand in it and in my heart, it was all to His glory. At that time, I wasn't bold enough to speak those words in any of those conversations. I was afraid of being rebuked. I was afraid of being mocked. That fear isn't gone, but it doesn't stop me.

When we moved into our current apartment overlooking a sparkling river, in a building with the exact architectural features I'd described, in a location walkable to numerous delightful businesses, some folks said, "This is manifestation in action." But I knew it was the answer to an open-hearted prayer that I'd prayed, that God had led us directly to this spot, and He deserved the glory for the blessing. I don't like to argue with people or refute a point they're trying to make, but gradually, I'm finding my voice to express my real truth. I know the blessings that flow to me are in response to my willingness to participate and because they're God's will for my life.

I would give all of it up tomorrow if it's what He wanted for me. I only want to be close to Jesus and to live my life for Him. Blessedly, that's exactly what I'm going to do.

Burn Up My Idols

In the past few years, I can admit that I had a selfish will. I was so self-consumed that I could not make room for God. There is a song called "Preference" by Rachel Morley that talks about missing God's presence because we want to reason Him away. The lyrics say "Offend my mind and reveal my heart. I want Your fullness, not just my preference." These struck right to my core because I needed to be offended so a light of truth could shine on the darkness of my selfishness. Now, I know that I want His fullness more than I want to be safe or to be right.

I spent a large leg of this journey deciding that I would custom-design my own personal version of God, one that was cozy and comfortable. The voices all around me encouraged me to do that, whatever I wanted! While it's fine to embrace our imaginations, we can never forget He is the one who created us and His ways are always higher than ours.

Yes, I was greedy. I convinced myself that I could and should have it all. All this stuff, the living God that my Christian friends spoke passionately about, and the secular self improvement-ism, plus all the New Age-y woo woo, I wanted it to co-exist easily and equally. I had conversations with many people who see Jesus as a historical figure, a wise philosopher, a great teacher, or just a generally cool guy. That felt manageable, right?

It's like one of those old TV specials where someone has the best, most devoted friend but because the friend isn't a 'cool kid', the lead character goes back to school and shuns them in the cafeteria. The character is just a human being, wanting it all, their wonderful friendship AND the approval and acceptance of the crowd. Still, it's not fair and it's not sustainable.

I kept asking God, c'mon, couldn't this be the way for me, too? Can't I just have Jesus as one of many "spirit guides", like when I talk to my departed grandmother's spirit? Does it need to be all about putting Jesus in the center of my life, declaring him

Lord and savior, the author of my freedom? Can't we just leave the provocative and controversial name of Jesus out of this whole thing? C'mon God, don't You know that I am supposed to be enjoying my life over here? It felt like enjoying life meant I should focus only on ease.

As I moved along, God's answer kept coming through loud and clear. His answer for me was no, we can't leave Jesus out of it. Jesus is the whole point. He has answered emphatically over and over, for many years now, it's Jesus. Jesus IS the way. This is where I am now.

I have simply resonated with the resurrection. As I returned to what Scripture says about Jesus rising in triumph over all sin and death forever, it was real for me. The way that I'd felt spiritually dead then resurrected into glorious life right here on earth made it personal. I remember saying the words, the victory of Jesus is my victory! It's mine - He died so I could have it, too! I feel this into the marrow of my bones. In choosing to follow Jesus, something supernatural happened and I was transfigured, and I can no longer deny it. I no longer even want to hide it.

Every lyric about streams in the desert, beauty from ashes, graves into gardens, ruins coming to life, it is all personal for me. There is nothing more true than a redemption and resurrection story.

A song by Eleventh Hour worship say, "The King is coming. He's burning up our idols." This strikes a deep chord in me. However well-meaning my pursuit of Enjoy Your Life has been, I've gone astray along the way. My attempts to worship at the altar of myself, of self-improvement gurus, of the stars and planets, all left me cold, empty, mired again. When I tried to stand on them, they evaporated like that spider web from the Book of Job, like a mist of dew drops vanishing in the sun. These things may have a place but it's not at the front and center of my life, my work, and my decisions.

I've loved a particular concept lately. It's the idea that in order to experience God, we have to trust Him and surrender to Him. And to do that, we must let go of all other things that command our attention, distract and enchant us. I'm easily distractible but I can claim a new identity. "Land of the Living" by UPPER-ROOM refers to the goodness of God "taking captive every lofty hindrance." I smile every time because I don't know exactly what a lofty hindrance is, but I'm surrendering mine anyway.

I saw the author Jennie Allen writing about the same subject on Facebook recently. She put it very simply, God will not compete. He has designed us and given us free will. He has given us a choice. We can worship at the altar of any false or worldly idol we choose. We can worship jealousy, doubt, resentment, or fear. Whether we decide to make Him the center of our lives is up to us. I've tried it all ways, and His ways are best.

I'm not condemning New Age spirituality or its possible role in a path to freedom for others. Maybe I should be, but I'm not ready to do this. Remember in the beginning of the book when I promised to be honest about what I know and what I don't? I don't know if following Jesus means a full strike-through for things like astrology or Human Design. I know that many are combining a Christian ministry with, say, the Enneagram. I believe it can be done for someone else, but it doesn't call to me so it's not what God wants for me.

I believe God can and does use many things to lead people home. He used many tools to support me along the way, including the years I spent in traditional talk therapy in my 20s and 30s. I have friends who believe in God and also use things like energy work and Reiki in taking care of their health. There are MANY things in this world that I can't explain and I know my inability to explain them doesn't negate them. It's not my business how God is showing up in other people's lives - I don't want the role of judge. In fact, a huge part of my freedom is finally understanding that I don't have to judge others because it's God's job.

I actively pray to have my impulse to judge pruned away from me. I surrender it willingly and ask that it be cast out. Judgment fuels resentment and resentment threatens to trap me back in the Mire. I want freedom!

For my personal spiritual journey, I have prayed instead for clarity. I have prayed for discernment around whether my New Age explorations should remain part of my walk. As I've done this, I've received strong signals that New Age spirituality divorced from Jesus and His resurrection is not a path that will lead me to deeper freedom. I just cannot dabble in the ways of Jesus.

I've come to see it's like sitting on the edge of a swimming pool with just your feet in the water, wondering why the splashing swimmers are having such a euphoric experience. You have to dive all the way in. A walk with Jesus requires a leap of faith, then calls for wholehearted dedication. And as these other distractions have been pruned away, as I've unclenched my hands and released them, I feel more free.

So, post-pruning, or rather mid-pruning, I'm writing from an increasingly wide open space in my life. I feel like a blank page or an empty bowl, spacious and ready to receive. In His pruning, God has stripped me of most pieces of my old story. I don't identify with the sad parts of my childhood or my young adulthood. I don't walk carrying my previous career failures. I don't claim shame over the financial mistakes I've made, nor over my divorce. I identify with resurrection power, with having conquered sin and death, with having been born again and made new. I identify with the God in whom all things are possible and my future is an exciting (if sometimes scary) clean slate.

I want to make clear that in addition to the satisfactions of Permission, Possibility, Participation and Praise...there is Pruning, which though painful, confusing, and lonely, is also satisfying. Though I've been confused over and over, I emerge from each episode with greater clarity. I've been profoundly lonely and yet,

I'm comforted by the knowledge that I've never been alone and never will be.

All of this strengthens the skill of surrendering, laying it all down. Through surrender comes deeper faith, through which comes greater freedom. In this way, every experience in life, beautiful or difficult, is an opportunity to be closer to God.

I believe in Unbelievable Freedom more with every day that passes, and for that, I praise God!

Submitting to God's pruning is part of the path to Enjoy Your Life.

CHAPTER 8

Pitfalls

Stumbling into Struggle Ruts

ENJOY YOUR LIFE gets tripped up and trapped in pitfalls. Learning to live a life in the fullness of joy just isn't linear.

For a long time, I explained this through the lens of Gay Hendricks and his book *The Big Leap*, in which he puts forth a construct called Upper Limit Problems. It's a well-written book that helped me during an important phase of my journey. In a nutshell, it's about the human tendency to move backwards, to return to the familiar. It attempts to explain why we do self-sabotaging things when we feel uncomfortable and unfamiliar levels of happiness.

I get tired of talking about struggle. It's tedious. It creates a yawn-out-loud level of boredom. I've done a ton of struggle talk because more than anything, I want people listening to me (reading me) to believe that I get it. I'm a struggler; it's wired into the way I was made. Struggle can feel like a shadow, something that always follows me even though I understand what it is and what it isn't. Struggle can come out whether the sun is shining or it isn't.

I want to leave the struggle behind, or at least to develop a certain immunity to it. Praise is like an infusion of vitamins but still, I stumble. I want to recognize struggle when it's happening and release it without resistance. I practice but because struggle is an aspect of human existence, I accept that I won't be fully without it on this side of Heaven. Much better for me is learning to sway with it, to dance with it, rather than thrashing and flailing against it. As I said earlier in this text, I employ gentleness because struggle can only exist in the presence of opposition. As Lao Tzu said, those who flow as life flows need no other force.

Struggle ruts are triggered by seemingly small things, words spoken to me, a flash of a memory, an uncomfortably familiar situation. The familiarity is what makes it dangerous, the twisted comfort of feeling the way I felt for so long, the siren song of the old story about who I was and what was meant for me. Whatever the trigger may be, it sets me into a spiral of thinking and feeling like old, mired me. I'm headed back in before I even realize what's happening.

A main way that I trip up and end up in a struggle rut is through comparison. It happens when I compare my life to that of others, or even through comparing my life to where I thought mine would be by now. I know I'm not alone in this, but it's been useful to call out comparison's role in triggering a struggle rut. I can usually catch it quickly and hold it up against what I believe about God and His promises for my life. It's usually the trappings of the world (status, money, etc) that cause this pitfall. It's helpful to think of my grandmother who possessed almost nothing enviable in the world's terms. She had a humble house and some utilitarian possessions. She lacked fortune or fame of any kind, yet she had everything.

Getting caught up in a struggle rut is sinister in nearly-invisible subtlety. When I'm going into one, on the surface, I look exactly the way I do when I'm inhabiting my real identity, the one filled with the power and authority Jesus has given me. It may even look like I'm doing Poster Girl for Contentment stuff. I might be sitting in the coffeehouse, latte by my right hand, but inside, the struggle rut is taking hold in the form of disempowered thoughts, things like "It's never going to work out" or "I'll never maintain a happy life" or "I should just give up." It might even be a thought like, "No one is going to read this book."

This is a reason why I love praise as an instant-access interrupter. I love turning to songs with lyrics about casting out untruths and breaking every chain. The darkness in my thoughts felt like being under a curse but I always had the ability to refute these lies. It took time to see them for what they are, but now I'm free.

"There is a Power" is a song by Rita Springer and these words resonate powerfully:

There is a power
There is a presence
Holding all heaven
Watching the earth
It can part troubled waters
Quench every thirst
Heal what is broken
And break every curse
There is a power
So overwhelming
All of creation
Bows to its name
It came to save every captive
Cover every stain
Keep every promise
And break every chain

Having given my life to God, specifically having accepted Jesus as savior, resonating with His resurrection as a personal victory, I still struggle. I am a human being with all the inherent frailties. I wish things could make sense or that my walk with Jesus could be easier. I feel weary and whiny at times, thinking about how much misunderstanding, misery, and divisiveness come into any conversation where the name of Jesus is uttered. Sometimes I don't want to deal with it and find myself wishing

I could just go back. Can you imagine? Wishing to leave expansive joy and freedom to go back to the mire?

These thoughts need to be taken captive and cast out because they're not of God. God didn't create me to feel weak, shamed, scared, or lost. When I have these thoughts, I know it's some other dark thing at work. And when I recognize it happening, I can give myself permission to have a wisp of a wallow, to take extra gentle care of myself, to acknowledge sorrowful feelings that are part of healing from my old straying. I can tell God I'm sad about all the time I spent turned away, and He will make beauty from those ashes.

My Mind Belongs to Heaven

Anxiety itself is a pitfall. I've experienced symptoms of what we call "anxiety" all my life. I felt deep, persistent, gripping anxiety long before I had ever heard the word. When I was too young to even articulate how I felt, it became my baseline and my normal. If you ask me how I felt as a child, my answer is that I felt afraid. A lot.

To this very day, there will be times when my stomach's in knots and my mind is racing and though it's not pleasant, it's familiar. I have felt anxious for so long that I have to work to see it as a thing separate from my true self. It reminds me of complaining about our cold, snowy weather and having someone say, but aren't you used to it by now? Being used to it doesn't make it enjoyable or nice!

"God of Peace" by Nikki Moltz is a praise song about overcoming anxiety that contains the lyric "My mind is not a playground where fear can come and go. My mind belongs to Heaven....". This resonates with me as well. I need to cultivate my mind the way one cultivates a garden, weeding away what is harmful, fertilizing what I want to flourish. My grandmother's words took root and sprouted, and the thoughts that grow out of that fertile ground are the ones that sustain me.

My weeping is one sign I'm still mourning for the years that I spent believing I was separated from God even though I wasn't. I still feel the pain of those sad, scared, lonely times. I give myself the grace to feel the feelings while stepping up in power, rejecting disempowered thoughts as the lies that they are. While I still weep for sadness, more often I weep out of pure joy, overwhelmed by freedom

There is a pitfall for me when I let food become too much of my focus. I've now maintained my 80+ pound weight loss for four years. Considering the statistics that tell us nearly 100% of people who lose significant weight regain it, I am proud and also grateful. Still, the subject of maintaining my weight loss can become a pitfall if I let it. I can slip into old patterns of mindless eating or binge eating sweets. Doing so makes me feel physically unwell, and triggers thoughts about my capability and my purpose. Food struggles feel familiar just like anxiety. Struggle separates me from God and connects me to my old false identity. It's a pitfall I need to stay vigilant against.

I can trip myself up by looking for the next "thing", the next guru. Our world is obsessed with chasing shiny objects, and I'm not immune from falling into that trap. While we believers know that a relationship with Jesus is exciting, ever-evolving, shiny and radiant, it isn't perceived this way by the world at large. We can fall into the trap of thinking like the world, imagining that Jesus is only part of old ways, old thinking, or dusty old churches. He isn't, but this can become a pitfall nonetheless.

Approval seeking can become a pitfall. It can feel like if we claim Jesus, we'll immediately be misunderstood by almost everyone, and disapproved of by many of those. Well, that's actually true; it is what happens and we need to be pruned of the need to be understood or approved of.

Another pitfall is telling yourself you can't speak up or live your faith out loud if you haven't figured everything out. That is a big part of what has gone on in the past couple of years as I backed myself into a corner as a micro-influencer in the weight loss sphere. For the longest time, I was posting my before-and-after photos, or sharing a picture of my dinner plate, talking about wellness and nutrition, but feeling I was "not allowed" to mention God. I feared someone would call me out and say hey, what do you know about God? I told myself the conversation was for - who? People of longer-standing belief? Less wobbly faith? Someone who has all the answers? No. That's yet another lie.

I am surrendering my timidity. Being timid is a trap. Timid was the fuel for resentment, which widened the separation between me and God. Believers are called out into a bold faith, a wild faith, where we share the truth that's being revealed to us without fear and with confidence. I've been overtaken by this truth, swept up in it. It indeed emboldens me in all areas of life. Every day, it seems, I'm having another opportunity to speak the truth of what I believe and how I see God's role in the circumstances of the world and other people.

Beware the False Dichotomy

Somewhere in my self improvement travels, I picked up the phrase "Take a Stand for the And." It was a reference to the idea that in so many situations, It's not either/or, it's both/and. If we want to flow, we need discipline AND surrender.

I went through a phase where I was focused on the surrender part - as miraculous healing began to create seismic shifts in my life, I was exhilarated. I wanted to just lean in. Feel the freedom. Let God take over. Bask in the abundance of His love. See beauty everywhere. Weep for joy. ENJOY MY LIFE.

Then I began to be equipped to do the work, to suit up for spiritual battle, I suppose. I went to church, sought spiritual mentors, and started following Jesus-focused social media influencers. I got overwhelmed and faith started turning into something that was too much, too hard, not for me. I started stealing my own joy.

I'm working to reject that I have to ricochet from expansive free-dom back into rigid discipline. I reject the idea that God doesn't want me to be this happy or doesn't want my life to be this good. Just as when I'm in the presence of my children and grandchil-dren, joyful to see them happy, the Lord delights in pouring out His love on us. He does want me to be happy; He wants me to be close to Him. I'm His joy and His pride!

The idea that God wants me to suffer is old thinking. I don't receive it. He has told me otherwise. I believe Him and I believe His promises.

Every day, there's another opportunity for old thinking to take over and tell me that other people are doing it right while I'm doing it wrong. Sometimes this comes up around the subject of church, a long-standing debate in my life. I've attended Catholic Mass, I've attended Protestant services, I've attended nonde-nominational/Contemporary worship. I've found value in all of them but I don't have a church home in my new city yet.

As I walk around town, I appreciate the energy of the old build-ings. Old factories filled with the energy of decades of work-ers creating, earning, providing. Old multi-unit homes filled with the energy of generations of families, caretaking, children growing, memories being made. Old churches filled with the energy of countless people seeking the face of the Lord. Walk-ing and delighting in this flow is a form of worship for me.

I especially love beautiful Catholic churches because they're part of my spiritual legacy, since my mother and her mother and her sisters were all faithful attenders of Mass. I'm grateful I know the beauty of Mass with its kneeling, standing, genu-flecting, reciting - the rituals are woven into me. Like I said, I make the sign of the Cross when I pass a traffic accident, a silent blessing on anyone who may be hurt and those tending them. I even do it when I see road kill. It's reflexive and instinc-tual to make this blessing. And while I understand the marketing behind "Catholics can always come home", I haven't been called back there.

One distinction that greatly helps me is what Graham Cooke calls having a habitational relationship with God and not just a visitational one. Church can be a part of the visitational piece but not having a church won't obstruct the habitational one. While I know many devoted Catholics have an active relationship with the Lord at all times, others simply use Mass as a way of checking something off the list. I know I don't want that to be me. Whenever and wherever I worship, I have to feel joy. That's my barometer.

I'm reading the Bible right now, in the spring of 2021. Simultaneous with the writing of this book, I'm reading cover to cover for the first time in my life. I'm nearly through the Old Testament, which in itself is amazing since I'd carried a story that I do not have the attention span to succeed in such a study. I told myself I wasn't disciplined enough to dedicate myself to reading a book of that scope and length, even as I did so with dense academic books many times over.

There was some kind of fear underneath it, I'm sure. I was around Bibles all my life. My mother gave me a Living Bible that I carried with me through all the moves of my 20s and 30s. It contained a neat table to cross reference your current trial to specific Scripture references. Over the years, I referred to it, made notations in a few places, but I never read the whole thing. I had no ritual around sitting down with it on a regular basis. I'm not sure what I was scared of, but it sat on a shelf unopened during many years of struggle.

One night right after my grandson was born, I had a really bad day. There had been a swirl of stressors and there was a heaviness resting on me and over the whole family, it seemed. As I was driving around despairing, I was overcome with an urge to drive to the local Books-A-Million, which I knew had a large selection of Bibles of various translations and styles.

I gave myself permission to buy any Bible that called to me. I spent the whole evening sitting on the floor in an upstairs aisle, pulling Bibles off the shelf, turning them over in my hands, flipping their pages. I bought a large hardcover New International Version with a floral design and a wide ribbon bookmark.

I started reading the Bible the next morning and have continued to read for 30-45 minutes every morning. I've read over 600 pages of the 1600 page text, and Ryan recently remarked that he doesn't think I've read 600 continuous pages of anything in two decades since he met me. This is the power of submitting to the Holy Spirit for me. I responded to the urge to get a new Bible and in turn, I asked to be equipped to use it and let it change me. I trust whatever's happening in me and around me as I read. It is another place of intersection between discipline and surrender.

The biggest pitfall I face is resentment itself. I am learning to recognize resentment for what it is: my ultimate obstacle to God. It is a false idol. When I descend into resentment, I feel a bitterness that tells me lies about who I am. It lies about who God is and what His plans are for me. Resentment is the road back to the mire. I have to stay keenly aware of the pattern. People pleasing sets up a cycle of self betrayal, dissatisfaction, and resentment. I must avoid people-pleasing behavior so I stay out of resentment and its Mire, so I stay close to God and walk in His freedom.

I surrender my resentment again every day. I ask that it be incinerated like a classic Old Testament burnt offering. Burn it up, Lord, and bring beauty from the ashes and freedom to my soul.

We can all avoid the pitfalls by recognizing the shadows in our lives and what they represent. We can claim a new life at any moment we choose. We can claim it over again. Born again? Yes, and again, and again, and again.

The curse on my old life has been broken, but the shadow is still there. I need to remain vigilant to my old sin nature and the lies that want to deceive me into returning to it. The Mire can pretend it holds safety and comfort but it lies. Worshipping at the altar of bitterness may be easy but it's a trap.

Enjoy Your Life requires a pitfall navigation plan. Walking closely with God will reveal the pitfalls for what they are, and He will help us steer around them so we don't fall in.

CHAPTER 9

Perseverance

Wait Upon the Lord

ENJOY YOUR LIFE will depend on perseverance and endurance to carry us through. When truly tragic things happen, we need a hefty dose. As Scripture says, we must wait upon the Lord and He will renew our strength. Weeping may endure for the night, but joy comes in the morning (Psalm 30:5).

Seated comfortably on my new La-Z-Boy in my dream apartment, sun filtering through the blinds, I'm keenly aware I haven't suffered to the degree that some have in their lives. There's been disappointment and despair. There have been divorces and deaths. But overall, I feel fortunate to have escaped the genuine trauma and abuse that many are enduring while I clack away on the magic keyboard of my iPad Pro, my slippered feet elevated on my suede recliner. Especially in the United States, we have the privilege of relative peace and prosperity compared to some places in the world. While I don't take it for granted, it didn't prevent suffering in my soul.

When I separated from my first husband, I was so broken. All the pain I'd repressed through my childhood and teens came crashing into full perception. Everything I'd done to go through the motions and pretend I wasn't struggling inside seemed to fall away. I made self-destructive choices and while they temporarily impacted my young children, I'm forever grateful that there were no permanent repercussions. My kids are actually what got me through that trial, and though they were too young to understand it, God was using them to show up for me. Knowing I was loved and needed by them gave me just enough purpose to stay alive when there didn't seem to be any other reason to do so.

While I now understand that my grandmother was also someone who loved, needed, and was praying for me, I avoided seeing her during the hardest part of that time. I was plagued by deep shame about having failed at marriage and even had thoughts about my divorce being a dishonor to her. I was so ashamed that I felt I could not bear to face her. I have to give myself grace when I think about times I could have gone to her but hid my face instead.

During my separation, she wrote a letter and mailed it to me. While she was a consistent sender of greeting cards, a full-length letter was a rarity. In it, she reassured me that she'd heard my sad news and recounted a litany of tough times in our family over the years, including my parents' (her son's) own divorce. She wrote these words that have stayed with me: "Some things just have to be endured." She closed the letter with the fact that she would always love me, something that would not change no matter what else did. I sobbed when I read it but it was a light in my darkness.

Until the time of her death, I viewed Gram the way a child views adults. I didn't think about what she'd endured or how painful many events of her life had been. I can now see that some of the trials her children and grandchildren went through pained her deeply. I cannot say how she may have coped or where her faith wobbled, but I believe she stayed out of any mire. She had her eye on the prize and she knew that her love and prayers were an active part of doing what she could and leaving the rest to God.

I admit I'm concerned about my current relationships and how they'll be impacted by my decision to live with wild & bold faith. It's one more place that I simply must trust. As I write and share the expansive freedom and joy of living committed to and focused on God, it gets easier to avoid the company of "scoffers" and "mockers." If people are mean-spirited or cruelly dismissive, I walk swiftly in another direction. If they don't even try to understand where I'm coming from, I release the need to try.

The hardest part is those who don't believe because of tough trials they've personally suffered. It seems trite to remind them that God is good in the midst of their agony. I'm tongue-tied when I encounter someone who says they cannot believe in a God who would allow so much violence, suffering, the death of babies or children, etc. Of course I understand that line of thinking. I spent a lot of my life with the same kind of logic, and my faith wobbled with each doubtful thought.

I'm so grateful to see the good being worked out in the midst of pain most of the time, but I never want to lose my sensitivity. I never want to say something that minimizes pain or gets received as a dismissive platitude. It's been a big part of my step into boldness to start speaking about what I believe, though I'm motivated to avoid offense to others. Sometimes I can't even engage in the conversation, but can only quietly lift this person up in prayer, asking God to reveal His nature to them in the midst of their pain, to Unmire them.

Evidence of Redemption

I don't begin to understand God's ways or His plan in redeeming some of those sufferings for His glory and our good. I only trust that it's His nature. I have seen evidence of His propensity toward redemption all over my life, like fingerprints, as they say. Some of these things take time to see, a lot of time, and the wisdom that comes from hindsight.

I've not only seen evidence of redemption. I am evidence of redemption. There's a song by Christ for the Nations Worship that says, "I'm dancing on the grave that once held me bound, I'm dancing on the chains that are laying on the ground." This is the best way to explain to anyone why I believe it will all be OK in the end. I've been given a Taste of Heaven (the name of the album from which that song comes) and once you've tasted and seen.... so it is. You can't un-know the truth. You can't un-feel freedom.

At this point, in terms of my own journey of life enjoyment, I want substance, not style. I don't endorse any of what is coming to be called out as toxic positivity. I am mindful that some things just suck....and those things just have to be endured. I believe God provides endurance to run that race. When things are the most crushing, purely and abjectly devastating, we have to lean way in and hold on tight. Picture what people do when a tornado rips through a landscape. They find a doorframe or get into the bathtub to hunker down and ride it out. You can, too.

God uses those same things we are enduring, if only in bringing us closer. He can bring us deep comfort in the very midst of it all, and His nature is revealed in those circumstances. They are used to teach us to rely on Him, which in the grand scheme, brings us even more freedom. For this exact reason, I am grateful for the Mire. It was a portal to my freedom.

I understand in a rational, intellectual way that if I am blessed to live many more years, I will endure many more heartaches. Pain is part of the recipe of living on earth and the fair trade-off for the kind of bliss we're allowed to experience here and all that awaits in Heaven.

With my weight loss story, I knew some might watch to see whether I regain the weight I lost. Similarly, those who've witnessed my faith journey from a relative distance may watch to see whether I endure life's trials with my faith intact. I don't need to figure out today how I'll deal with these hypothetical situations when they occur. I know my game plan, which is to rely on God and His promises.

Relying on God goes for the good and the bad of this life. He's never lost a battle, and thus, this plan never fails. Asking for His help lets you persevere and Enjoy Your Life.

CHAPTER 10

Pandiculation

Awaken and Expand

ENJOY YOUR LIFE will lead to pandiculation, a level of growth that stretches you far beyond what you've ever experienced before.

I debated whether I should use this obscure word that means "stretching upon waking." It is technically a term referring to the literal stretching of the physical body, an instinctive way of moving that humans do when they have just woken from sleep. It's used mostly in the context of physical therapy and kinesiology.

For me, and for this section of the book, I am claiming the term in a more metaphorical sense. When you awaken spiritually, when you receive an infusion of spiritual truth, how does that influence your next move? How does that cause you to stretch, reach, grow? For me, it has inevitably created a swell of courage, a wild new boldness. This awakening has been accompanied by a desire to use spiritual fuel to expand even further, to pass the energy on to others. It is making this the most thrilling chapter of my life.

At this moment in my life, I am truly stretching. I'm talking about BIG stretches. Just being here on the page, in any public platform speaking about Jesus, is a huge stretch for me. It's something I wouldn't have done a few years ago because I abhor confrontation and controversy. I've never wanted to make any proclamation if there was any chance I could be wrong. I recall leaving a test question blank because I wasn't 100% sure and did not want to guess, feeling anything was better than being... gulp...wrong. This intense need for certainty before acting has gotten me stuck in the past, but now I'm in motion.

I'm in action. I'm talking. I'm using my voice, if tentatively, in public forums about my journey and the role that Jesus has played in helping me heal, making me whole, giving me authority to walk in boldness over timidity. This is pandiculation-awakening and stretching - if anything ever was.

Whether it was people pleasing or simply avoidance of discomfort, I've been non-confrontational to a flaw. From that place, I worried that my assertions of faith would be triggering for others. I remember so many points along my own journey when someone else shared their faith boldly without fear or shame and I was triggered in some sense. I now understand it to have been an "anointed annoyance", placing grains of sand in my spiritual shoe. As I come forward to speak about my faith journey, my efforts may have this effect on others. I accept it.

Followers are departing from the small rooftop that is my online platform. Some are expressing their displeasure before they go. It is a stretching of my new spiritual boldness not only to accept this fact and continue to show up in my truth, but to send my prayers in each person's direction. My only desire for others is that they experience the freedom for which they were born. The role I can play in that comes from my testimony, my story and my song.

Professionally, what we call "career" is something I'm turning over in my hands and investigating with new eyes. I've allowed my career (or lack thereof) to be a source of shame for a long time and I now reject that shame. Instead, I'm setting bold new goals. I'm speaking out into the world that I intend to publish this book in the months to come. When it's finished, I'll put it out there as it is, with the admitted hope that it will be a success in both income and impact. I want a lot of people to read this book. I don't know who they are, who YOU are, but God does know. I trust that He is already preparing certain hearts and making ways for this book to move into specific paths.

Part of this pandiculation grows out of my awareness of my grandmother's legacy. Whether she felt stretched or it came easily, she was able to leave a powerful impact on the world by the way she showed up. I want that. The idea that one day my children and grandchildren will say, "We understood and received the abundant, life-changing love of God because of how Mom showed up, because of how Kiki adored us" - this makes my breath catch in my throat. There is nothing I want more, no greater honor that I can picture.

As I see it, I'm drafting my own job description in this phase. Sarah Blondin is an author and speaker who has a podcast called "Live Awake." At the same time that its broad spiritual focus may be deemed New Age, it has a lilting, beautiful message that resonates with me. I have received healing through its words and I'm grateful for that. Like Sarah, I deeply desire to Live Awake for the rest of my life. I'll call it a requirement for success in the work I've been called to do.

The current chapter of my life is called Becoming Kiki. Kiki is my "grandmother name." It was suggested or said by one of my Grand Girls - my son's stepdaughters - when we first met. It immediately felt right, like slipping on a sweater that just fits, so it stuck. It's funny because names are such an important subject. My grandmother was very traditional about names, and I'm told she wasn't in favor of Kimberly as a choice for me. Perhaps it seemed a little trendy, and I'm told that she disliked its prominent connection with the famous Kimberly-Clark toilet paper company.

In any event, the parents are the ones who choose a baby's name, and my parents chose to name me Kimberly Joan. I trust we're all given the name we are meant to have and I've embraced it. I've gone and back between Kimberly and Kim over the years, and of late, I have proudly and simply decided to be Kim Smith, a forgettable name but an unforgettable person.

There were times when I thought about how my trajectory might have been altered by having another name. I thought about having been named Joy, what a blessing that might have been, to have Joy claimed right within one's own name. Various names held the favorite spot at different times, including things like Alexandra and Caroline, until it was time to choose names for my own children. I named them Adam Chandler and Emma Lorraine, and my Gram referred to me as "the mother of her namesake" until the last of her days.

Now, Kiki feels like a name I was meant to carry. I claim Kiki and I step up into it more and more as the months pass. As for officially becoming a grandmother, a biological grandmother here at age 47 ½ years old, it has been a beautiful if truly unexpected blessing.

It was a huge surprise to learn that I was going to become a grandmother in the summer of 2020. It came at a moment in my life when I least expected and most needed it. I was JUST getting my bearings after the years I spent raising my children. Those years overlapped the deeply challenging ones in the Mire, but as I've already referenced, my kids were bright lights in my darkness. I loved them with such ferocity that I wondered where those feelings came from. I now know that love came from God. I also know that, just as all the cliches claimed, the love I have for my grandson is even stronger than what I had for the kids. The more I receive God's love, the better I become at giving it away.

News of grandmother-hood also came in the midst of a pandemic, during a time when I was wondering if any of us had a future. We were all living in a bit of a survival mode at that time. I was listening to Kari Jobe's "The Blessing" with the lyrics about God's favor being on my children and their children, but I could barely get beyond the day we were on. I certainly wasn't imagining a new baby coming into our family and bringing big dreams for an expanded future.

My Wonder Boy

One of the reasons this book has been on hold over the past couple of years? God knew grandmother-hood was going to stretch me in big ways that needed to happen first. I needed my Wonder Boy to enter the scene. This is the nickname I've given to my grandson Colson, barely two months old, because of the spiritual lessons I've learned since I found out he was joining our family. Awe at his existence quickly felt exciting and very right. Just like that moment outside Dr. Starks' office when God whispered He'd always known what I needed in my work, the baby news was God winking at me.

One day early on in the adjustment, I was fretting over the stress a new baby can bring to a young couple. I was slipping into a struggle rut when I was suddenly overcome with the sense that my grandmother, who loved babies and was intensely proud of her family, knew she was becoming a great-great grandmother. I remembered her pride the day my son Adam, her first great grandson, was born.

With this revelation, I felt suffused with her joy and was left with a deep sense of peace. I had a feeling that I could only describe as: Gram says the baby will help our family heal. I repeated this to others. I spoke it out and claimed it, and it's already happening.

Then, during early scans, the doctors discovered that the baby had some exceptionalities. The first indication was the discovery of a condition called situs inversus. This means the positioning of his internal organs is reversed, a mirror image of what is typical. Most noteworthy is that his heart is on the right side of his chest rather than the left, thus he is literally "right hearted." This feature is part of a syndrome that was not diagnosed until genetic tests were performed in the days after his birth. It is officially classified as a rare disease and its implications are still being figured out.

Actually, the doctors will do what they can (and I'm grateful for each one of them) but I have peace that God has it all under control. This is what I mean when I say my unborn grandson was healing me. He was teaching me broad spiritual truths before he was even born. It was when these issues started emerging that God spoke and told me to trust Him with Colson's life. While I'd likely said the words that God is always good and He is always in control, did I believe it? I'm not sure, but I know that learning my first grandbaby could have significant medical complications brought it home like no other lesson could have.

As someone who experienced significant anxiety about each and every aspect of raising her own children, to be at peace about a grandchild is noteworthy. To be at peace about a grandchild with a rare disease is even more awesome. This tiny boy has a cardiologist, a gastroenterologist, and a pulmonologist already. He has seen more specialists in his brief life than I've seen in all of mine. And yet, rather than fearful, I feel peaceful. I believe Colson has been knit together in this unique way for a reason, and while I don't know what that reason is, I trust it. This is freedom.

Likewise, God is revealing Himself to my son Adam through these circumstances. I sheltered both my kids from religion because of baggage from my own childhood church experiences, and they didn't grow up with much talk about God until they were in their teens, coinciding (not surprisingly) with the events surrounding the loss of their Great Gram B. They were blessed to have her in their lives until they were 17 and 14. Though she was equally quiet on spiritual matters in her conversations with them, they felt from her all that I felt from her. She stood in for God with them, too.

While I surrender any illusion of ability to control the process, I see my kids as "pre-believers" because I can feel God drawing them nearer to Him. I see it at work all the time...how can I not? They've watched my rebirth and they are reluctantly accepting the way I talk and the bold prayers I'm compelled to speak out and over them. It's a joy when they ask me for more of the prayers I'm already praying.

While only God knows His plans for them, I expect and claim that they will come to believe and feel the freedom I do. I'm grateful for new interpretations of God's word and His will so I'm not compelled to moralize at them. My story and the way God has worked in it shows me that He is a way maker and will make a way for them to access Him in the right timing.

In the meantime, it has been humbling to watch Adam express seeds of faith over the circumstances surrounding his tiny son. I'm so proud of who he is becoming as a husband and father. I'm grateful to hear of him sending up any prayer, even a clumsy or uncertain one. Sometimes those are the best ones of all.

It is satisfying to see my daughter Emma's dreams for her life and career coming true. She has been the textbook definition of a joy to raise. She always has a smile on her face and brings a gentle, cheerful energy into a room. Her very presence soothes me. In so many ways, she represents what my grandmother did then, and I love her so much that it hurts. During the writing of this book, she graduated from college and moved away to the "big city" to start a fancy new job. I helped her move then sobbed all the way home. I will miss having her close by but wish her all the joy that she's brought me in the past 22 years and then some.

My daughter-in-law Makayla is evidence of God's ways at work. She's a gentle and loving person who also reminds me of my grandmother. It wasn't until she came into my son's life and they formed a family together that I realized I'd been holding my breath. Because his developmental path has been so unique, I hadn't been willing to dream into possibility for him. I knew he wanted to be a husband and father, yet I'd held back from dreaming of it. God knew all along that He had created Adam for a mighty purpose, a plan that involved a gorgeous baby Wonder Boy with so much more in store.

The day I was invited to accompany Makayla to one of her ultrasounds, I sat in the darkened room with tears pouring down my face. I could not believe the miracle that was this tiny boy, so uniquely stitched together, his right-sided heart beating away on the illuminated screen. I was just awestruck, a miracle before my very eyes, and a strong sense that God was at work more powerfully than ever in our family's circumstances.

Then when Colson was born, I was cracked open like never before. Yes, this is corny but it's true. It's something that grandmothers tend to say, and a phenomenon of which I was readily warned. Friends who'd already become young grandmothers told me that the love for a grandchild is stronger than even the love they felt for their own babies, and now I can echo them. It is one of the most powerful things that has ever happened to me.

My first glimpse of Colson after his birth was through video chat. There he was, impossibly beautiful with dark hair, full cheeks and a dimple in his chin. I was smitten. Enchanted. Enraptured. I wanted to gather him up under my wings to protect him from everything forever and simultaneously, I wanted to shout it to the rafters, turning myself into a walking grandmother's brag book, holding up my iPad to show his photo to strangers who didn't even ask.

Visiting the hospital was impossible due to Covid restrictions, but the week after they came home, I was able to travel back to my hometown where my son still lives to spend a few days holding and admiring the baby. I'm lucky to be self employed with the ability to put my work aside and just bask in the glow. As I drove home after that visit, I was listening to (you guessed it!) praise music, including the song "This is a Move" by Tasha Cobbs Leonard. The words struck a deep place inside me, and I broke out in tears as the truth washed over me. I still get goose-bumps remembering it:

Mountains are still being moved
Strongholds are still being loosed
God we believe, 'cause yes we can see it
That wonders are still what You do

And in that moment, I decided I would call him my Wonder Boy. He came into my world after a few years of seeking God earnestly, at the end of a pandemic that had seen me surrender to God's will for my life, including death, and during a time when I was waking up to miracles all around me. And here was one held in my own hands! I wept for joy and made a commitment that I'll always show this child how wonderful he is, how wonderful God is, and how much joy there is in store. I'll be right there with an "Enjoy Your Life" at all his ages and stages.

I can't speak for others but in my case, I know the overwhelming power of my grandmother-love is because of my relationship with God. Understanding even a fraction of the abundant love God has for me equips me to love others more powerfully. Maybe this was my Gram's secret, too. Likely that overflowing well washing over me as I stood on the hot-air register was a product of her relationship with God and the blessed assurance she had. She is my role model in how to be an impactful grandmother and an ambassador of Heaven.

I would like my work from here forward to lead others toward the freedom I've discovered. I am not sure what form that will take but I'm available and I'm here for however God wants to use me.

My Upper Room

At this moment in my life I'm stretching and stretching, growing to be someone more than I've ever been, claiming a whole new identity. I claim being Kiki as a robust, holistic way of showing up in the world. Kiki is someone who is secure in herself, in her freedom, and in her relationship with God. Kiki is someone overflowing with love that impacts not only her husband, children, grandchildren, but everyone with whom she interacts. Kiki is kind and generous, Kiki is easily delightable. Kiki often has her hands raised in praise, and nearly as often, she weeps tears of relief and joy. Kiki is who and how I want to be, and so it is. Kiki enjoys her life, just like her Gram taught her to do.

Of course, there are ways my life is NOT mirroring my grandmother's at all. Gram stayed in her jam-packed house until the end of her days on earth. I'm half of the age she lived to be (almost exactly! 47.5 is half of 95!) yet I've already let go of the family homestead where the children were raised. The freedom & simplicity of our minimalizing, of living in and from our streamlined "Upper room" is another important part of Becoming Kiki. I'm giving myself the freedom to admit that I'm not going to rock in a chair and wait for the grandchildren to visit. I'm trusting God that I can have Gram's contentment without limiting myself to a static recreation of her entire lifestyle.

I know my faith doesn't look like my grandmother's. It is wild and loud, demonstrative, full of singing and waving my hands. As time goes on, I'll say more about the way it feels emotionally to have been led out onto the water in this way. It feels like the old me/false me continues to be poured out. Each bit that is poured (or pruned!) makes more space for joy. It helps me become the vessel that I want to be. For now, I'll leave it with these lyrics from "One Who Stays" by Summit Sounds [feat Nikki Mathis]

So take my life like the wind takes an empty sail
And my heart, soften it without fail
You make my heart go wild
You make my heart go free

I'll keep a laser-like focus on my identity and on my legacy. James Clear's incredibly popular book *Atomic Habits* posited that our habits flow from our identity. We don't do behaviors that are incongruent with the story we tell about who we are. Therefore, by making Kiki the centerpiece of my identity, I am giving myself a great context for how to live. I used to joke that there was a variant of What Would Jesus Do? called, What Would Gram Do?.

Gram displayed gentle ways to show up - how to be kind and generous to others. I often look at how she lived and the way she managed to enjoy her simple, humble life. Now I can add the very similar question, What Would Kiki Do? Who Would Kiki Be?

The answer is, Kiki is a trophy of God's grace and she does whatever aligns with that. She's filled with joy and freedom so most people like to be around her. She isn't needy or manipulative. She has no agenda for others except to enjoy them, and with them, her life. Kiki loves others in a way that helps them understand God's love. Kiki releases struggle for the sake of staying in flow, asking for and receiving constant support from God, Jesus, and the Holy Spirit.

When you think about pandiculation, think about your legacy. What do you wish for it to be? I hope it doesn't sound morbid, but I really do think about how I want to be remembered. My kids have several same-age peers who have already lost their mothers to cancer, and that loss is part of what some must endure. I imagine how I want those I love to speak about me after I'm gone. Even before I moved into deep faith about Heaven, I'd say I wanted my kids to memorialize me by saying, "Remember Mom? Wasn't she great?" Now I wish for much more than that. I want my life to feel so much like freedom that they pursue it for themselves.

I don't know if my grandmother had these thoughts in advance. I cannot tell you whether she thought I might revere her enough to miss her every day for eight years, enough to write a book about and for her. I only know that she set a bar for me to pursue. Honestly, as I watch my tiny grandson grow and thrive, he feels like the most influential person in my ongoing journey. He is making me into that bar-setter. For him to later say, "My Kiki taught me about what's important in life", that's my idea of personal success.

While I have ambitions to write and sell books, to create inspirational content with my photographs and snippets from my meandering-and-musing, more than anything, I want to make God proud. I imagine arriving at the end of my life and Him saying, Atta girl. You were everything I made you to be. You struggled and you persevered. You lived well and you led others toward home, toward Me.

If you love Jesus and you are seeking to live like Him, there is no greater blessing than to understand that how you treat others helps them see Him. THIS is my grandmother's legacy in a nutshell. I could have skipped writing the entire book by saying, my grandmother lived like Jesus and it showed me how to live my life. But I thought it would be more fun to tell you all about how it unfolded, and I was right.

The following section is going to give you just a few guidelines for making Enjoy Your Life a mantra for your own days.

CHAPTER 11

Process

ENJOY YOUR LIFE is an active, moment to moment, fully engaged process. In order to trust the process, we have to trust God. To truly enjoy life, we need to live with intentional focus on God's presence in every moment and every circumstance. When we seek it, we find it, and it guides us. At least, that is the powerful experience on which I based this book.

As I referenced at outset in Promises, this section on Process provides a little bit of guidance for moving from contemplation into action.

Create your own process that supports a daily Enjoy Your Life flow. Create it using discipline - personal practices and rituals - and wrap it in all surrender to God's will. Pepper in plenty of delight. Delight brings in the magic. I echo Graham Cooke in that I "delight in the Lord as a lifestyle."

In my mind, the ultimate goal of this process is to live with a faith that is broader + bolder. It's all about how to receive deeper responsiveness to the Holy Spirit in our daily workings. It takes practice, plain and simple.

I will leave it to other authors and teachers to direct your steps in terms of studying the Bible or living the teachings of the Gospel. I don't feel far enough along in my walk to give that kind of advice but I know open-hearted prayer will lead you to the resources you need. This is a layer of Participation - finding the people who are sharing their stories, making speeches and sermons, writing books, performing music, and generally shining light in the world. They are being used to call others home, each in his or her unique way.

If you deeply desire true spiritual freedom, I believe it is available to you. I can only base my guidance on my own experience, and that experience leads me to say that you must make your relationship with God your very highest priority. You must initiate a genuinely active, intimate communication that exists above any other in your life.

I look to God as a way to flow through every circumstance. I ask God to help me make decisions for my career. I ask Him to help me show up better in my marriage, my family, and my community. I understand that He created me and that my life and everything in it belongs to Him, and I seek deeper alignment with His plan and His will with every day that passes.

I also ask the Holy Spirit whether I should or shouldn't "pay it forward" when the person in the car in front of me paid for my Starbucks. I close my eyes and in a millisecond, I've asked without asking and am given a nudge in my heart to say yes or no. I don't have to analyze my budget or wonder whether that stranger is or isn't deserving. I have my answer, I make my action, and I move on. This is the flow.

Ask. Receive. Pray. Surrender. Find the flow. Find it again. And again.

Each and every single time you realize you've exited the flow, use these as the points of re-entry: Permission. Possibility. Participation. Praise. Hint: Praise is the quickest way back in for me!

Are you giving yourself permission to Enjoy Your Life, remembering your own Divine design and what God promises His children? What could be holding you back? What are you pretending not to know?

Are you dreaming into possibility, understanding that the desires of our hearts were placed there by God and He wants to help us reach them? Do you believe that any dream that's dying or dead can be resurrected?

Are you participating with the Spirit in an active way, knowing we can do all things with Him? Are you acting, moving, and getting willing to be uncomfortable?

Are you praising as though you were designed to do it? There will be times of simply waiting on the Lord, but you can worship in your waiting. You may not feel like you're going anywhere, but at least you are not going astray.

Are you keeping the good and bad in perspective? Are you willing to surrender certain parts of you, to let God prune them away? I believe that in the pursuit of Enjoy Your Life, there will be Pruning; there are things God will want you to release as His plan for you unfolds.

Likewise there will be Pitfalls, many of them self-constructed and able to be self-deconstructed. A huge part of what's given me such freedom is recognizing how struggles that ruled my life were based on lies and illusions. As I've healed, much of it has disappeared, but the residue remains. We have to be vigilant about not falling backward because miry clay can be slippery.

Toughest of all are the things we must endure with Perseverance. There is so much value in just being held during times like that. Our trust deepens with every surrender. Though I've only endured a few of these tests of faith, I believe you can and that God will be there for you every step of the way.

Pandiculation means awakening and stretching into a legacy that will last beyond your time here on earth. You can choose to write the rest of your story in any way that feels good. You are in charge of how you live and how you are remembered.

I hope that after you've read so much of my story, you can receive my assertion that belief is a decision, one you can choose at any time. A recent devotional that I read on social media worded it this way: Realize that the Lord is already here and the freedom is immediate. It is truly this simple for me. I spent many years of my life witnessing my grandmother's faith and aching to have it for myself. It was right in front of me yet a million miles away. I created and maintained that distance, and when I changed, the distance closed and my unbelief vanished like a puff of smoke.

Whenever someone I know has a loved one pass away, I think of my grandmother in Heaven, of course picturing the same petite old woman that she was at the end of her life. In a half-kidding way, I tell the person that my grandmother probably volunteered to be on Heaven's Welcoming Committee on her first day there. I can clearly picture Gram warmly greeting newcomers, noting any connection and chatting away in delight. In the same way that she framed our visits around catching up, I see her getting caught up with each old and new friend as they are promoted to the Glory.

It brings tears to my eyes because in those moments, I see her as vividly as when she was still alive, and I know I will see her again. It feels like Heaven will be some version of me standing on a hot air register, hearing her humming nearby, knowing she's a few feet away making pancakes or whatever Heaven's equivalent is.

Believing this truth is what I requested when I beseeched the Lord to deliver me from my unbelief. He has granted it, along with more freedom than I thought possible. He has given me all that I ever needed or wanted. He has given me new eyes and a refreshed spirit.

I thank God for giving me my Gram, and I thank my Gram for giving me God.

All my life you have been faithful
All my life you have been so, so good
With every breath that I am able
I will sing of the goodness of God
"Goodness of God", Jenn Johnson

I believe God will faithfully abide with me all the days of my life.

I believe in Unbelievable Freedom.

Post Script

To know You and to make You known
This is the anthem of our souls
Send us out, we will go
Anywhere you lead us Lord

"Driven by Love"
Lindy Conant-Cofer and the Circuit Riders

I hope reading this book offers you a new perspective on God and the way He works. I'm one imperfect human woman but His offer of freedom stands for all. To know Him and make Him known is the anthem of my soul.

You have my deep and sincere gratitude for reading. Other than raising my children, this book is the most important project I've ever tackled. You are helping me carry a legacy for my beloved Gram.

I thank my family for supporting me, especially when I'm over-flowing with emotional expressions of faith. Sometimes what is happening in me is so strange and uncomfortable, I can hardly imagine how it feels for others. I trust it all, and I appreciate the love and acceptance they've given me in the process.

I believe my future work will, in some way, involve people on a journey similar to the one I'm on. I do not know what that might look like, but God does. If you want to stay connected as time goes on, find me on social media @unbelievablefreedom or on the web at www.unbelievablefreedom.com

Believe in Unbelievable Freedom! Enjoy Your Life!

Kim "Kiki" Smith
May 2021

Made in the USA
Middletown, DE
10 June 2021